BFI FILM CLASSICS

. . . .

Rob White
S E R I E S   E D I T O R

Edward Buscombe, Colin MacCabe and David Meeker
S E R I E S   C O N S U L T A N T S

Launched in 1992, BFI Film Classics is a series of books that introduces, interprets and honours 360 landmark works of world cinema. The series includes a wide range of approaches and critical styles, reflecting the diverse ways we appreciate, analyse and enjoy great films.

Magnificently concentrated examples of flowing freeform critical poetry.
Uncut

A formidable body of work collectively generating some fascinating insights into the evolution of cinema.
Times Higher Education Supplement

The choice of authors is as judicious, eclectic and original as the choice of titles.
Positif

Estimable.
Boston Globe

We congratulate the BFI for responding to the need to restore an informed level of critical writing for the general cinephile.
Canadian Journal of Film Studies

Well written, impeccably researched and beautifully presented ... as a publishing venture, it is difficult to fault.
Film Ireland

FORTHCOMING IN 2002
. . . .

Ivan the Terrible
Yuri Tsivian

The Manchurian Candidate
Greil Marcus

Mother India
Gayatri Chatterje

October
Richard Taylor

To Be or Not to Be

Akira Kurosawa on location during filming of *Seven Samurai*

BFI FILM
CLASSICS

SEVEN SAMURAI
七人の侍

Joan Mellen

bfi Publishing

For Donald Richie, of course.

First published in 2002 by the
BRITISH FILM INSTITUTE
21 Stephen Street, London W1T 1LN

The British Film Institute
promotes greater understanding
and appreciation of, and
access to, film and moving image
culture in the UK.

British Library Cataloguing-in-Publication Data
A catalogue record for this book is available from the British Library

ISBN 0–85170–915–X

Series design by
Andrew Barron & Collis Clements Associates

Typeset in Fournier and Franklin Gothic by
D R Bungay Associates, Burghfield, Berks

Printed in Great Britain by Cromwell Press, Trowbridge, Wiltshire

CONTENTS

'SEVEN SAMURAI'

. . . .

Seven Samurai is 'the best Japanese film ever made', Donald Richie wrote in 1965. His judgment of Akira Kurosawa's 1954 masterpiece remains as valid today. The discomfort of the generation of Japanese film-makers which followed Kurosawa's, particularly that of Masahiro Shinoda and Nagisa Oshima, promoted Kurosawa's temporary fall from critical favour. All that has now changed. Formalist critic Noël Burch has been proven prescient in his description of Kurosawa as 'the one true master which the post-war Japanese cinema has known'. No single film-maker in the intervening years has earned comparison.

One might go further. Even Ozu and Mizoguchi, the great directors who were Kurosawa's contemporaries, but who came of age in the Japanese cinema of the 1920s and 30s, fall short of Kurosawa's stylistic range and the breadth of ideas in his films. Kurosawa stands as a transcendent artist who, for Japanese cinema, is the measure against which all others must now be compared. *Seven Samurai* is his finest film, the apotheosis of his style and the most complete, subtle and powerful expression of his world-view. Repeated screenings only confirm its original impact.

Great works of art in the epic mode command a high place in the history of civilisation: those who risk this form have been few. Cinema, the newest art, with its unselfconscious capacity to traverse wide vistas and space, has, however, inspired artists – the Soviet directors of the 1920s foremost among them – to chronicle the historic fate of entire societies, cultures and communities. At their best, as with *Seven Samurai*, they locate themselves at moments of historical transition.

An old culture – an entire epoch – approaches its inexorable demise. A nascent social order struggles to be born. As the story unfolds, we witness a tumultuous emergence. The values of the old era, and those of its embryonic successor, are observed and weighed. The strength and vitality of the new are juxtaposed to the decline of the old, even as what is being lost is evoked. As the past retreats, the narrative prepares us for a future rendered newly accessible to our understanding.

Sergei Eisenstein's *The Battleship Potemkin* (1925) is one of those films, and the single strongest influence on Kurosawa as he made *Seven Samurai* was Eisenstein. *Seven Samurai* embodies Eisenstein's classic formulation of montage, the collision of shots which reveals a third, synthesising meaning. Simultaneously in *Seven Samurai*, Kurosawa accomplishes for his society what Eisenstein achieved for his own.

Kurosawa, for his part, evokes the cultural upheaval which followed the fall of Japanese militarism in the sixteenth century, no less than that of the moment in which he made the film, the aftermath of the American Occupation. Despite the apparent liberating environment accompanying both these moments of social change, there was a dramatic attendant diminution of the national identity.

Some have thought that Kurosawa was a Westernised (hence less authentic) Japanese director because American Westerns, at their best, reveal values emerging from that transitional moment, the conquest of the West. Howard Hawks's *Red River* (1947) and John Ford's *The Searchers* (1956) and *The Man Who Shot Liberty Valance* (1962), as well as Robert Altman's *McCabe and Mrs Miller* (1971), share with *Seven Samurai* the epic impulse. Kurosawa acknowledged early the seminal influence on his work of John Ford, although his films are more parallel to Ford's than they are directly a result of Ford's style and outlook. If Kurosawa has acknowledged, with grace, the influence of both Ford and Hawks, *Seven Samurai*, at its core, has little in common with the American Western.

The plot of *Seven Samurai* is deceptively simple. A village of farmers has suffered the annual encroachment of a group of forty ruthless bandits, who steal the harvest, kidnap the women and wreak general havoc. In desperation, under the guidance of the ancient village elder, the desperate farmers decide, improbably, to hire samurai to save their village. There had never before been a Japanese film in which peasants hired samurai, or an evocation of the social upheaval which made credible such an idea.

More accurately, the farmers seek disenfranchised samurai, or *ronin*, those warriors set adrift into the society. Without a master to serve, they are themselves starving and without occupation. Six *ronin*, and one would-be warrior, aided by the farmers, whom they train, save the village by killing all the bandits.

There is a leader, Kambei (Takashi Shimura), who expresses the height of samurai integrity and patriarchal selflessness. His counterpart is Gorobei (Yoshio Inaba), a man like himself and an intellectual. Kambei's loyal 'sidekick', Shichiroji (Daisuke Kato), joins the group.

Among the six is a samurai, Heihachi (Minoru Chiaki), who expresses the capacity for open-hearted generosity with which, at its very best, Kurosawa associates this class. There is a master of the sword, Kyuzo (Seiji Miyaguchi), who personifies traditional samurai skills. Finally, there is the youth, Katsushiro (Ko Kimura), who comes of age in his ardent pursuit of a consuming desire to become Kambei's disciple at the very moment when Kambei has become disillusioned and weary of a life of endless combat. He can ill afford an apprentice.

Kambei embodies samurai modesty, expressed not in words but in gesture. He rubs his shaved head throughout the film at moments when praise would embarrass. 'You're overestimating me,' he tells Katsushiro. 'Listen. I'm not a man with any special skill.' If he has fought in many epic wars, these have been 'losing battles – all of them'. Self-effacement is a redeeming and vanishing trait, evocative of samurai integrity for Kurosawa. Kambei expresses it in full measure.

Each character is distinctly complex and individual while exemplifying a facet of samurai virtue. Kikuchiyo is the character who stands at the emotional heart of the film. His peasant origins and rebellious transformation into an iconoclastic warrior express the epic moment of social transition at the heart of *Seven Samurai*. Kikuchiyo is played by Kurosawa's signature actor, Toshiro Mifune. He is accepted as a samurai out of the passion, energy and the intensity of his desire which transcends the social impediment of his class. That the bandits who prey on the peasants are themselves *ronin* contributes to the dramatic irony which suffuses this film and highlights the theme that overwhelming change presses people into roles they would not otherwise assume.

'You're overestimating me,' Kambei tells Katsushiro

Kurosawa's abiding admiration for the dedication of the samurai class at its most authentic permits them to become heroic not merely in battle. It reflects, too, his respect for his father, 'a strict man of military background', as he would write later in his *Autobiography*. The family traced its ancestry to a famous Genji warrior, and as a child Kurosawa's father still wore the topknot, the emblem of the samurai class. As a teacher at a gymnasium, the senior Kurosawa was a man with 'a single-minded devotion to discipline'.

He was a strict father who would rap his younger son's knuckles with the heavy ends of his own chop sticks if Akira happened to hold his chop sticks without grace. Kurosawa's mother, who was from a merchant family, was upbraided if she served fish pointed in an incorrect direction. Her driven husband went so far as to accuse her of wanting him to kill himself since she invariably placed the fish in the manner appropriate to those about to commit ritual suicide. As a boy, Kurosawa absorbed his father's stern ethos and took kendo fencing lessons, a choice which pleased his elder.

Paradoxically, Kurosawa's father was also a man of his time, one who loved the movies, which he said had 'an educational value'. He combined the liberal enlightenment of the samurai class with its rigour and self-discipline. Despite the family's strained circumstances, he did not object to young Akira's ambition to be a painter. That Kurosawa's brother was a *benshi*, a narrator for silent films, allowed Kurosawa to merge his interest in painting, in literature and in music into one artistic form.

Seven Samurai is a classic epic transcending even the limitations of that genre. On the surface an action drama of men in conflict, it rises to the level of tragedy. The heroism and the debilitating flaws of a class are dramatised through the emotions of seven individuals. The apotheosis of its conclusion, as in all tragic works, comes complete with a final, cleansing catharsis.

Yet, transcending narrow definitions of genre, *Seven Samurai* is so replete with satiric scenes, verbal jokes, wit, irony and broad humour as to qualify as a great work of comic art. Frequently, the humour is conveyed solely in visual terms. After tripping through a meadow of wild flowers while the other samurai are hard at work, Katsushiro, ignoring his temporary youthful self-indulgence, spies a young peasant. Katsushiro demands to know why he isn't drilling. To underline the point to the seemingly reluctant youth, he gestures, pontificating with the bunch of wild flowers he had just picked and which reveals his own frivolity.

In this scene, Kurosawa draws on the theme of disguise and the transposition of identities, a standard comic convention. Wrestling with this reluctant recruit, Katsushiro discovers her gender. 'A girl?' he asks suspiciously, pulling his hand away in horror as if he had touched fire – as indeed, the virginal young samurai has done. In another such satire on the impermanence of identity, Kikuchiyo boldly dons samurai armour to fool the bandit whose gun he will soon confiscate. Kurosawa's inherent optimism, a quality demanded of comedy, emerges in the ease with which Kikuchiyo can impersonate a member of the samurai class.

Throughout, Kurosawa's use of the comic relies on irony, as in the futility of farmer Manzo's (Kamatari Fujiwara) attempt to keep his daughter concealed from the samurai whom the farmers themselves have brought to the village; the old grandad is sardonic in summing up the social crisis which propels peasants to take unprecedented steps in order to survive: 'What's the use of worrying about your beard when your head's about to be taken?' he asks Manzo.

Much of the humour revolves around Kikuchiyo, whose role in itself is absurd: he is a samurai in courage, wit, selflessness and strength, all but in manner and the lowness of his birth. As Kambei realises – he is no samurai, but a 'farmer's son'.

That he has so many of the qualities claimed by the samurai themselves is conceded by Heihachi: 'So now we're seven, eh!' This comes as a triumphant comic moment in which a man rises out of the limitations of his class to fulfil the possibilities contained within him. Kikuchiyo is also given a gesture parallel to Kambei's rubbing of his head: Kikuchiyo runs his finger under his nose at moments when he is embarrassed.

When the fearful farmers refuse to leave their houses, Kikuchiyo's laughter resounds. He is the only one laughing. He is consistently engaging, for he illuminates the stuff of comedy: the capacity of the human character for transformation.

Yet he is also a 'low' character, described both verbally and by his gestures as a 'dog'. 'A dog is luckier,' one of the townsmen comments, referring to farmers. 'He's like a wild dog,' another tells the farmers, reporting excitedly that he has found them another samurai. Kikuchiyo kicks dirt behind him, like a dog, when the peasants refuse to emerge from hiding to welcome the samurai. Kikuchiyo calls the bandits 'wolves', as later one of the farmers will also call the bandits 'worse than wolves'.

The dog imagery of *Seven Samurai* is benign when compared to the angry canine at the beginning of *Yojimbo* made seven years later, in 1961. The world of Tokugawa Japan has diminished appreciably in a moral sense since the sixteenth century. It is an era characterised for Kurosawa by senseless violence borne of greed. The merchant class has gained ground, a harbinger of Japan's future. The canine of *Yojimbo* is a real animal, a relative of the menacing black dog with his teeth bared who appears in extreme close-up under the credits of *Stray Dog* (1949), set in contemporary Japan.

In *Stray Dog*, that fierce beast represents the villain, a 'mad dog', a psychological casualty of the Pacific War. In his diary this criminal reveals that he killed a cat because its purring annoyed him, adding that the cat was 'worthless' like himself.

As Donald Richie notes, 'the detectives see him as a mad dog; he sees himself as a worthless cat. Dogs chase cats and cops chase robbers. By association, Mifune [the cop, the good guy in film] is the dog.' The suggestion is that the cop and criminal are not all that different.

Vicious and an emblem of a community beyond redemption, the dog in *Yojimbo* runs down the street with a human hand clenched between his teeth. 'The smell of blood brings the hungry dogs,' an observer comments, as gang warfare prefigures the merchant-infested Japan of the twentieth century.

In *Seven Samurai*, the people co-exist with animals, even as hostile, normally conflicting classes co-exist in an uneasy alliance, indicative of a rapidly disintegrating order. The association is captured by Kurosawa in a slapstick scene in which Kikuchiyo attempts to ride farmer Yohei's tired, sagging and ancient nag. The horse gets the better of the man. The scene will be reprised later in the samurai raid on the fort when Yohei's horse leaves Kikuchiyo behind and, suggesting their shared qualities, he must plead for the animal's forgiveness.

'Please,' Kikuchiyo begs the horse. 'Forgive me!' The animal imagery is, for the most part, gentle. Kikuchiyo earlier had called Yohei's horse playfully 'a fat mouse'.

Kikuchiyo's animal qualities establish his links to the farmers and to the earth. He dies like an animal in the mud, the rain beating down on his unclad body. As Donald Richie notes, evocatively, 'he lies on a narrow bridge, on his face, and the rain is washing away the dirt from his buttocks. He lies there like a child – all men with bare bottoms look like children – yet he is dead, and faintly ridiculous in death, and yet he was our friend for we have come to love him.'

Kurosawa enlists animal imagery for all his characters, not only the farmers. They are dubious whether samurai would help them. 'Hire *hungry* samurai,' the old grandad tells them. 'Even bears come out of the

forest when they're hungry.' Rikichi's (Yoshio Tsuchiya) hideaway resembles a 'bear's lair'. People in crisis are reduced to essentials. History had taught everyone a harsh lesson and neither class feels any great sympathy for the other.

In terms of traditional Japanese genres, *Seven Samurai* is the quintessential *jidai-geki,* or period film. Set in the past, it exposes the meaning of history, enlisting for its surface action the lesser form of the *chambara,* or sword film. It encompasses both high and low, the grander dimensions of the *jidai-geki* and the less demanding pleasures of the *chambara,* the Japanese B-Western.

Yet like *Ikiru* (1952), the other of Kurosawa's masterpieces – and a favourite among his films – *Seven Samurai* is no less a 'home drama', or to use Ozu's term, an *Ofuna-cho,* named after the studio where Ozu worked. Born of the *shomin-geki,* home dramas were about 'people like you and me'. Kambei is not merely a samurai leader, a warrior of consummate military accomplishment, but a man who has grown old in service without fulfilling the ambition of his youth to become a 'warlord'.

Kikuchiyo is distinctive as the man incapable of restraint, the member of the group whose every emotion is visible. Heihachi, the wood-chopping samurai, is a 'fencer of the Wood Cut school', a reference to Japanese *ukiyoe,* or woodblock prints. Although he is only a second-class fencer, he has other virtues: by nature he is cheerful, and his 'gay indifference' and insouciance are a consolation to all. Rikichi, the farmer whose wife was abducted by the bandits, is an everyman, whose character deepens with his suffering. Samurai and farmers emerge as 'people like you and me', their fates personal and domestic no less than cosmic. Only the bandits are flat, one-dimensional characters, having completely surrendered all standards and moral restraint.

The family emotions, the fabric of domestic travail, of the *Ofuna-cho* are also present. The samurai become a family in themselves and then integrate themselves within the wider family of the village. In Katsushiro's reverence for Kambei resides the respect of son for father. Katsushiro's admiration for the cool ascetic discipline and skill of Kyuzo captures the source of inspiration where the young discover their own strength. Katsushiro's passion for farmer Manzo's daughter, Shino (Keiko Tsushima), contains the universal defiance of young love, a passion which transcends class, history, time or expectation.

Farmer Manzo's conviction that his daughter will be seduced by one of the samurai, so much more dynamic and attractive than her fellow farmers, is the stuff of the home dramas, as is her fear that her love for Katsushiro is doomed: 'You're a samurai and I'm a peasant,' she tells Katsushiro. The inculcated peasant fear of the superior class is also expressed in personal, emotional terms. Only when Kambei has cut off his topknot and shaved his head, divesting himself of the outward signs of his samurai status, can the farmers summon the nerve even to bow in the dust and make their appeal for samurai support. 'We don't know anything at all about samurai,' one acknowledges.

Heihachi chops wood, while Gorobei, seated, makes a proposition

All of this occurs within history – the time when the film is set – and the cultural moment when Kurosawa made his film – the aftermath of the American Occupation of Japan.

'Seven Samurai' and Japanese History: The Individual and the Group
Most *jidai-geki* are set in the Tokugawa period (1603–1868), a time of relative peace when the country was unified under a single shogun. For *Seven Samurai*, however, Kurosawa, chose the Sengoku period. It began in 1467, the beginning of the Onin War, a bitter dispute between the Hosokawa and Yamana houses which the shogun was unable to mediate, and which continued until 1568, the date when the warlord, Nobunaga Oda, entered Kyoto, marking the beginning of the reunification of Japan.

Sengoku meant 'Warring states', and the country was in perpetual turmoil. The period was more properly called *Sengoku Jidai*, The Age of the Country at War, a term from Chinese history in which individual warlords battled to the death, a chaotic period which lasted for more than a century. Kurosawa has located his film at a time of change and turmoil, with the future of the entire society, and its survival as a unified state, in question.

Clan fought clan, and *daimyo* battled *daimyo* for land and power. The country shattered into autonomous territories, each ruled over by a *Sengoku-daimyo*, or military family. A *daimyo* would employ thousands of samurai, professional warriors of a hereditary noble class called *bushi*, whose attachment to a clan or *daimyo* signalled their legitimacy.

The title opening *Seven Samurai* is a synopsis of all that follows: 'The *Sengoku* Period was a time of civil wars; it was a lawless era and in the country the farmers were at the mercy of bands of brigands.' Kurosawa adds an historic parallel: 'Around the time of the St Bartholomew's Day Massacre in France, in the sixteenth century, Japan was in the throes of Civil Wars. And the farmers everywhere were being crushed under the iron heels of cruel bandits.'

His comparison with the French Wars of Religion in the sixteenth century is apt; with the Protestants moving ever closer to the throne, and national unity at stake, the monarchy executed the Huguenot military leader, Admiral de Coligny. On St Bartholomew's Day more than 3,000 Huguenots (French Calvinists) were murdered. Twenty thousand more perished during the next three days. Thirty years of civil disorder accompanied the rupture of the iron hold of feudalism. With the dreaded Protestant cultural challenge to feudal autocratic control emerged hitherto unimaginable aspirations towards personal freedom.

As in Japan, so in France the national fabric was being rendered and a series of seven civil wars erupted lasting until the final decades of the century. In France, without the bond of a single faith (*une foi, un loi, un roi* – one faith, one law, one king) it was feared the entire social order was at risk; in Japan, as the centralised authority of emperor and shogun gave way to clan warfare, the very notion of the state was put in question. It was an era in which the rise and fall of great houses assumed centre stage.

The very opening of *Seven Samurai* reveals the absence of civil authority. In the first sequence, the farmer, Mosuke, suggests that the villagers take the problem of the marauding bandits plundering their village to the 'magistrate'.

'What's the use!' he is told. 'He'd come only after the bandits are gone!' In sixteenth-century Japan there is no longer a viable central authority, no reliable civil governance. Government officials are entirely unresponsive. A woman says in desperation, 'let's give everything to the bandits and hang ourselves. That might get some action out of him.' At a moment of social anarchy, in the people's utter inability to invoke authority, taking the law into one's own hands becomes the only option.

When a *daimyo* lost one of these wars, his castle was burned and his lands were confiscated. His samurai were cast out into the countryside to live by their wits. Some got themselves hired, selling their skills to new masters; warlords like Nobunaga raised armies of tens of thousands of warriors. He took 200,000 such fighters on his ill-fated venture into Korea. Other samurai, less fortunate, roamed the countryside in search of any means of survival. You were part of a coalition army, or you were frozen out. The conquered rivals of the great Nobunaga surrendered their castles and their samurai became *ronin*. The worst of them, like the bandit tribe in *Seven Samurai*, survived exclusively by preying on the most vulnerable.

Meanwhile, during almost a century of civil wars, as feudalism became decentralised, there was already rising, as Kurosawa suggests, a merchant class which would supplant the warrior aristocracy. This is the theme Kurosawa would develop in *Yojimbo*, the conceptual sequel to *Seven Samurai*.

Another term applied to this period, as George Sansom observes in *A History of Japan, 1334–1615, gekokujo*, which meant 'the low oppress the high'. It dated from the preceding century and expressed the moment when the country was overwhelmed by 'discontented warriors seeking reward for their services', reflecting nothing so much as 'a disturbed social order'. As emperor and shogun lost their power to the rival warlords, so these warlords and their retainers intensified an unbridled repression of the lower social orders.

Kurosawa locates the unexpected benefits no less than the tragedy of this historical moment. The upheaval forces samurai to channel the selflessness of their credo of loyal service into working for peasants. It was, socially, a preposterous enterprise, as many of the samurai reveal in the marvellous sequence where the farmers come to town to enlist samurai.

'To fight whom?' and 'What clan?' are the samurai's responses to Kambei's proposition. These were the right questions. 'My ambition is a bit bigger,' this proud, if threadbare, samurai declares. The farmers despair. 'The strong are beyond our control,' Yohei reflects. 'Any who seem to be willing are weaklings.' Kambei concedes, 'it's not easy to find seven reliable samurai.'

Kurosawa's brilliantly elliptical command of history allows him to dramatise the entire sixteenth century, from the battles between warlords to the edict in 1590, when Hideyoshi froze the social structure and prohibited class mobility and change of status. *Bushi* were prevented from leaving one master for another or from settling in villages; peasants were restricted from entering the trades or commerce.

In *Seven Samurai*, the characters all live within this history. They are portrayed simultaneously as individuals and as members of a class. Despite the violence and upheaval which might predict social transformation, Japan looked forward to the rigidities of the bureaucratic Tokugawa period when rules of behaviour for each class were strictly enforced. The prospect of upward mobility, of transcendence of one's class, would be unthinkable. Kikuchiyo, in all but name, behaves as if he were a samurai, but historical authenticity demands that he does not survive the final battle of the film.

The world of *Seven Samurai* is one of constant warfare. With no powerful shogun at the helm, with a process of the rise and fall of powerful military families, the political unit has been reduced to one of armed men defending castles and the lands they hold in fief. Farmers, however, in the midst of this chaos, have been seizing the opportunity to create self-sufficient communities; in these decades of civil war they have only to ensure their own self-defence.

Ironically it was a time when the Japanese peasant prospered. He needn't report the true area of his land – there was no centralised system of checking – and he invariably offered false tax returns. A consistent land tax appeared only at the close of the century under the rule of Nobunaga's general, Hideyoshi, and then the peasantry resisted. In 1584, Hideyoshi was driven to threaten to crucify the men, women and children of villages in which false tax returns were made. He also closed in on the unruly *ronin* roaming the countryside by expelling after 1591 any *ronin* newly entering a village.

By the time Ieyasu Tokugawa, who had been an ally of both Nobunaga and Hideyoshi, consolidated his power at the end of the century, there were tens of thousands of disgruntled *ronin*; there were still 230,000 men in the field of battle, their efforts culminating in the Battle of Sekigahara (1600).

100,000 *ronin* were on the losing side alone in this final battle among *daimyo*. They fought for the Toyotomi family and Hideyoshi's successor, his son Hideyori. The victor was that old warrior Ieyasu, who had bided his time, and who had waited to consolidate his power, at the end ruthlessly destroying those loyal to Hideyori. In the Tokugawa period, with the civil wars finally over, many samurai became teachers or doctors, a fact reflected in Kurosawa's own family.

The villagers in *Seven Samurai* – murdering dying samurai who wandered onto their land, stripping them of their armour, hoarding food and sake – have become adept at survival, as Kikuchiyo reveals in the culminating moment of the first half of the film.

Kikuchiyo has discovered a cache of spears and superb examples of samurai armour hidden by farmer Manzo. He believes the samurai will be delighted with this discovery, for surely it can only help in their war against the bandits who themselves are well-armed. The six samurai are, in fact, appalled. 'I'd like to kill every farmer in this village,' Heihachi, normally benign, says in fury.

Kikuchiyo is puzzled, but Kambei explains: 'One who has not been hunted would never understand.' Thus Kurosawa expresses what will be an even greater antagonism between farmers and the military class in the years to come. Nobunaga's successor, Hideyoshi, restricted the bearing of arms to any but the *bushi* or samurai class; Kurosawa's peasants carefully hide the armour and weapons they have plundered. By law, peasants were forbidden to have in their possession: swords, short swords, bows, spears, firearms or other types of arms. In 1588, Hideyoshi ordered the peasants to turn in their weapons – he knew they had them.

The farmers are 'stingy, foxy, blubbering, mean, stupid and murderous'

Farmers, Kikuchiyo cries, are 'stingy, foxy, blubbering, mean, stupid and murderous'. He reveals their hidden arms. He has unearthed rice, salt, beans and sake! He knows that while they pose as saints, they are full of lies: 'But then, who made them such beasts? You did! you samurai did it!' In the wake of the great military campaigns of the age, women and children were slaughtered with impunity.

'You burn their villages! Destroy their farms! Steal their food! Force them to Labour! Take their women! And you kill them if they resist! What should a farmer do?' Five of the samurai are in the background of the shot. Only Katsushiro, who is too young to have participated in these atrocities, is absent. Kikuchiyo goes off to sleep in the barn with Rikichi where he will remain from now on. 'I don't like their company,' he explains.

Seven Samurai is, then, first and foremost an historical film, and in particular a film about the military. Kambei is a master strategist, as the montage of his movements from one end of the village to the other (West, South, East and North) reveals. 'Defence is harder than offence,' he knows.

Sixteenth-century Japan also chronicles a moment in the change of the Japanese style of warfare, herein recorded. Hand-to-hand combat between armoured samurai was yielding to foot-soldiers standing shoulder to shoulder in lines facing their enemies, armed with long pikes. Already by the sixteenth century, samurai had become an officer class presiding over foot-soldiers known as *ashigaru* (light foot). At times, even peasants were conscripted into battle.

This democratisation of the battlefield is reflected in the method Kambei will enlist in his battles with the bandits; the farmers will be the foot-soldiers, and since the bandits have stolen all the horses, the samurai, too, will be on foot. The style of warfare itself is creating new institutions, all of which will conspire in the obsolescence of the samurai.

Yet remnants of the old style remain. Just as the samurai are becoming obsolete, so is their manner of warfare. But these men, refugees from past days of glory, still embody traditional samurai skills. Kyuzo, 'a man interested only in perfecting his skill', belongs to the old school. Yet history, change and disenfranchisement have led him to enlist in the attempt to save the village. Even as he, more than any of the others, expresses the samurai ideal, he is condemned to live as a *ronin*.

Among the required skills of the samurai was archery, and Kurosawa credits two archery advisers for this film. Both Gorobei and Kambei, old-style warriors, take up the bow and arrow, and, unerringly, strike home. Because they too are *ronin*, the bandits are as accomplished with the bow and arrow. Meanwhile, nowhere more aptly does Kurosawa reveal the coming obsolescence of the samurai than in the presence of guns and gunpowder.

By the mid-sixteenth century, the Japanese were manufacturing muskets in workshops. The Dutch traders and the Portuguese had brought the new technology to Japan. More complex guns had appeared,

Old style warriors, Gorobei and Kambei use the bow and arrow with unerring skill

as well, in Japan. Kurosawa expresses his disdain by placing this new weaponry, the technology which foreshadows the Westernisation of Japan, entirely in the hands of the vicious bandits. Even when the samurai capture two of the three guns, they do not use them. Of the samurai who die – Heihachi, Gorobei, Kyuzo and Kikuchiyo – all are brought down by gunfire. As ideal examples of the samurai class – and this includes Kikuchiyo – they could not be defeated on their own terms.

Kurosawa's Themes

Seven Samurai is above all a homage to the samurai class at its most noble. Although realism appears to be its mode, Kurosawa lifts his discourse beyond surface action at every stage. Each of the seven may be individuals, but each is also an aspect of samurai identity, and together they reflect the history of the class and its coming demise. Samurai for Kurosawa represent the best of Japanese tradition and integrity and their passing from the historical stage is nothing short of the loss of the unique Japanese identity. Without samurai, Kurosawa implies, little is left of what it means to be Japanese.

It is a class by birthright; what you are born is what you will remain, even as the evolving society refuses your class a place. This is the condition faced by Kambei and the others, Kambei more so because he has lived at the moment of samurai power and must now confront its decline. As a man he is 'tired of fighting', a reflection of the historical weariness of the class. He has failed in his ambition to be a warlord and his biography reflects as well the sacrifice samurai made: he has lost his parents and his friends in the pursuit of his warrior life and warrior ambition.

Kambei is also, Kurosawa told me when I interviewed him in Tokyo, a samurai in whom something is 'missing' in the 'worldly sense'. The same is true of the others. 'They couldn't get jobs and further their careers.' That these outstanding men have not been hired by some *daimyo* expresses in itself a flaw in the samurai conception, which presages the fall of the class.

As he trains the villagers, Kambei expresses what Kurosawa defines as the most important of samurai ideals: that of selflessness. For the village to survive, three of the houses must be sacrificed, flooded to deprive the bandits of egress through the open fields. At dead centre of the film is the culminating scene in which Kambei (and Kurosawa, for whom he stands) offers the essential wisdom of the film. That Kambei speaks for Kurosawa, that his character offers facets of the director's own, becomes apparent.

Ending his *Autobiography* in 1950, with the international triumph of *Rashomon* and its winning the Golden Lion of St Mark at the Venice Film Festival, Kurosawa adds, playfully, 'look for me in the characters in the films I made after *Rashomon*'. (Ironically, *Seven Samurai* would receive only the Silver Lion, second prize.)

In Kambei, in his modesty, the concealment of his own doubts and the fortitude with which he refuses to admit the possibility of the bandits emerging victorious, is a figure remarkably similar to the man Kurosawa has described as himself: 'I am not a special person. I am not especially strong. I am not especially gifted. I simply do not like to show my weakness, and I hate to lose, so I am a person who tries hard. That's all there is to me.'

In Kambei, but in the others as well, Kurosawa portrays his own emotional spectrum. The samurai enable him to reveal his own private code, the values he cherishes. You can hear his voice as well in the scene where Katsushiro speaks of his admiration for Kyuzo to Kikuchiyo. Kyuzo has just returned from an extraordinary feat. He went off into the night, entered the bandits' territory, and returned in the morning with one of their guns. 'Killed two,' is all he says, and this only so that Kambei can keep his tally accurate.

Kyuzo emerges out of the fog: 'killed two'

Katsushiro is overcome with admiration for this ideal samurai as he had told Kyuzo that morning, 'You are ... really great ... I've always wanted to tell you how great I think you are.' This elicits a slight smile from austere Kyuzo.

'He has real samurai spirit,' Katsushiro gushes about Kyuzo some time later. Kikuchiyo pretends disinterest. 'He's fearless and skilful and also gentle. So modest even after capturing that enemy gun,' Katsushiro explains. Even as Kurosawa adds irony by allowing these words to be spoken by a very young, unseasoned person, they remain reflections of Kurosawa's own admiration. Kikuchiyo is inspired to abandon his post and capture a gun as well, a transgression which allows the bandits into the heart of the village.

Throughout, Kurosawa contrasts the two cultures: peasants, with the advantage of their usefulness to society, assuring that they will endure into the future, and samurai with their superior personal morality and elegance. The peasants pursue their sexuality without hesitation: it is Shino who seduces Katsushiro. The samurai express restraint. They have not concerned themselves during this war with the need for sexual release.

This is true even of Kikuchiyo, a farmer by birth, but now a samurai by teaching and by example. 'Who would have thought so many

Katsushiro praises Kyuzo while Kikuchiyo pretends not to listen

women lived here!' he cries out during the harvest which opens the second half of the film. It is, of course, only Kikuchiyo, part farmer, who could even raise the issue of his need for a woman. Feeling the same sexual urgency, Kyuzo silently goes off into the rain to practise – his version of the cold shower. The scene of the harvest in brilliant sunlight is also a reminder that the peasants are the ones leading 'normal' lives; even Rikichi had a wife before she was taken by the bandits.

Male friendship is another of the abiding themes of *Seven Samurai*. The friendship which develops between Gorobei and Kambei reflects the balm which renders life endurable. It is, like many, a friendship which arises spontaneously. Yet, as the film develops, it becomes a profound connection. Gorobei's decision to help save the village is not motivated by compassion, or pity for the farmers. He joins the expedition because, as he tells Kambei, 'your character fascinates me'. 'The deepest friendship often comes through a chance meeting,' Gorobei believes.

Kambei had spotted Gorobei as a kindred spirit even before Gorobei revealed his acute intellect, and before, despite his disclaimer, his sweetness emerges when, casually, he stops to observe a group of street urchins playing. 'Try him!' Kambei tells Katsushiro.

It is a version of love at first sight. Gorobei and Kambei will remain inseparable as long as both are alive in this paean to male friendship. 'Oh, Gorobei, Gorobei, Gorobei, Gorobei,' Kambei cries when he sees that his friend has been shot. It is Kambei's moment of deepest pain in the film.

Kambei and Shichiroji are renewing an old friendship during which, in many wars, Shichiroji served as Kambei's 'right-hand man'. It

Gorobei and Kambei talk at the inn: 'your character fascinates me'

23

is a connection leavened by their respective survivals, against all odds. Shichiroji remained alive, even after a burning castle tumbled down on him. Between such old friends few words are necessary. Among samurai, words are particularly superfluous. 'Were you terrified?' Kambei enquires. 'Not particularly,' Shichiroji answers. 'Maybe we die this time,' Kambei notes. At this, Shichiroji just smiles. They are, after all, samurai. In this unique 'home drama' the samurai immediately develop loyalty, admiration and love, each for the other, acknowledging and accepting each other's powers and foibles. *Seven Samurai* chronicles the consolations of male friendship, a theme which touched Kurosawa when, as a child, he saw the Westerns of William S. Hart. 'What remains of these films in my heart,' he would write in his 1982 *Autobiography*, 'is that reliable manly spirit and the smell of male sweat.'

It would seem that a friendship is developing between Rikichi, tormented by the loss of his wife, and Heihachi, the kindest and most open-hearted of the samurai. It is Heihachi who tries to draw Rikichi out and break down the barrier. 'You're a man of few words,' he begins. After this scene, Kurosawa includes Rikichi and Heihachi in the same shot, revealing that Rikichi has attached himself to this mildest of the samurai.

But any real friendship between these two, Kurosawa makes clear, is not possible. The film does not assess blame, but it is Heihachi who tries to stop Rikichi from rushing into the bandits' burning fort, and Rikichi who, thinking only of himself, at least in part contributes to Heihachi's being shot. Kyuzo had tried to hold Heihachi back, but in the chaos and because of Heihachi's concern, he failed.

The persistent metaphor of Kurosawa's work is that of wind, the winds of change, of fortune and of adversity. In his *Autobiography*, speaking of his brother's failure in the exam which would have led to his acceptance to Tokyo Imperial University, at that time ensuring a distinguished career, he writes that 'just as this desolating wind overtook my home, yet another cold gust of change began to blow'. He uses the phrase 'the winds of life' and, from the time he began to direct, the wind blows hard in his films. Gale-force winds rage in the climactic scene even of his very first film, *Sanshiro Sugata* (1943). The wind blows mightily in *Yojimbo* as well. In *Seven Samurai*, in one of many techniques which lift this film beyond its apparent naturalism, transcending realism as well, a driving wind surges through the action. It is a wind heralding the loss of samurai culture and the endurance of the peasantry.

In the town early in the film, Kambei states that selflessness is both pragmatic and the highest good. As the time for the battle with the bandits approaches, Gorobei, who is Kambei's alter-ego, offers a traditional Japanese perspective, contending that the individual must give way to the group. In the conflict between *giri* (duty) and *ninjo* (personal inclination), *giri* must prevail. 'We'll harvest in groups, not as individuals,' Gorobei explains. 'From tomorrow, you will live in groups. You move as a group, not as individuals.' The selflessness which permitted these samurai to agree to help a peasant village must now be inculcated in the farmers themselves.

Suddenly, Mosuke and a group of others rebel. Theirs are the three houses which will be flooded after the harvest and they are horrified. 'Let's not risk ourselves to protect others!' Mosuke yells. They break away from the group and rush off. They are only six, however, and Kambei, sword drawn to reveal the urgency of this moment, drives them back to be reincorporated into their units.

Kambei and Shichiroji

'He who thinks only about himself will destroy himself, too'

As he articulates this credo, Katsushiro accompanies him in the shot – Katsushiro, the youngest samurai who is learning what it means to be a samurai. Kambei moves, so that the reframing of the shot now includes Gorobei.

Kambei now expresses the ethic at the heart of the film. There are only three outlying houses. There are twenty houses in the village: 'We can't endanger twenty for three. No outlying house can be saved while the village proper is destroyed.' Peasants, who have always lived selfishly, must learn: 'That's war.' 'He who thinks only about himself will destroy himself, too,' Kambei says, moving to stand at the dead centre of the shot. He offers a lesson that moves beyond the particular history of the sixteenth century, to the present and beyond. 'Such selfishness will not be tolerated.'

Later history, with the advent of the merchant class, will reveal that it will not only be tolerated, but endorsed, a perspective which led to *Yojimbo*, with its satiric impulse and Sanjuro Kuwabatake's (Mifune's) remark that it would indeed be better if everyone in the town perished. His judgment offers a reprise of Heihachi's despairing remark that he would like personally to kill every farmer in the village.

The musical motif attached to the samurai now flares up. A long shot is substituted for Kambei. More important even than this superb leader is the group itself, the collective unit, with everyone lined up, spears in place. Through the cut and this substituting shot Kurosawa conveys the transcendence of common purpose as the first half of the film draws to its emphatic finish.

The divergent perspectives of these two cultures – samurai and peasant – remain a dominant motif. In the second half of the film, the wilfulness and individualism of the peasant culture is expressed through Kikuchiyo. The theme begins when Kambei and Gorobei go out into the night to examine their defences. 'The weakest first,' Kambei says. They happen upon Kikuchiyo sleeping so deeply that Kambei is able to seize his sword. Awakened, Kikuchiyo, still a peasant, gropes wildly for his missing weapon. As Kyuzo illustrates later, no samurai can afford to sleep so completely that he loses awareness of his surroundings.

Kikuchiyo's peasant individualism emerges again when the three bandit scouts enter the village. The samurai conceal themselves, hoping to retain the advantage of the bandits' ignorance that they are there. But Kikuchiyo gestures and shouts exuberantly, and the scouts discover there are now samurai in the village; the advantage is lost. They have no choice but to go after the three scouts.

Two are killed outright, for Kyuzo's sword is unerring. The third is taken prisoner. Expressing their ethical perspective, Kambei and the other samurai attempt to restrain the crowd of angry peasants from killing the prisoner. Although warfare is their *raison d'être*, there are rules which must be obeyed. 'This is a prisoner of war. We must not kill him,' Kambei says, as if he were fighting one of the wars of feudalism.

Mercy is not the farmers' way. Forever preyed upon, when their predators fall into their hands, they become, as Kikuchiyo explained, 'murderous'. On this occasion Kyuemon's granny, whose entire family was killed by the bandits, suddenly emerges with a scythe. The music becomes solemn. The old grandad orders the villagers to help her as haltingly she stumbles towards the captured bandit; there is no shortage of volunteers to help dispatch the prisoner.

Kambei chastises a bewildered Kikuchiyo

Kikuchiyo's last expression of his peasant mentality emerges in the scene in which, urged on by Katsushiro's hero worship of Kyuzo, he leaves his post to perform a similar act of bravery. Rushing off into the woods, he sniffs expressively, a reiteration of Kurosawa's association of this character with animal instincts; he moves by his sense of smell as he responds to the scent of the burning gun fuse.

'You fool!' Kambei chastises him when he returns expecting praise for his escapade. 'Why did you leave your post!' It is one more educational moment in the film, as the samurai attempt – and invariably fail – to infuse their values into those of the villagers. 'Going on your own merits no reward,' Kambei tells Kikuchiyo echoing his earlier speech to Mosuke and the rebelling farmers. 'In war, it's teamwork that counts.'

Subsidiary to this theme is the notion of how truth is to be taught. Katsushiro stands once more behind Kambei during this apocalyptic speech. It is argument by example that persuades. Kambei is what he preaches. Yet anyone can learn, even Kikuchiyo who is ordered by Kambei to 'Go, catch one of them to make amends,' after he has inadvertently exposed the samurai presence in the town to the bandits.

Later in the film the same Mosuke who had led the rebellion chastises others for mourning the burning of those houses which had been abandoned, calling them 'worthless shacks'. Kurosawa revered his teachers, in particular Kajiro Yamamoto, his mentor at Toho. The salutary image of an older person instructing the young evokes always in Kurosawa's films high moments of pathos.

Kurosawa's appreciation of the way of the samurai is nuanced. The history of the samurai has not been one of noble self-sacrifice – and the figures he presents here rise to moral excellence out of the social upheaval which has turned their rigid world topsy-turvy. The bandits offer a portrait of samurai brutality; by the last day of the battle the bandits have reverted to bows and arrows, as Gorobei had done, and as Kambei will.

Another of the film's great themes, then, is the ambiguity of class distinctions at moments of social turmoil. Throughout Kurosawa poses a dialectic, a running discourse as to whether a farmer can be a samurai, and hence whether class mobility is desirable, possible or inevitable as societies are transformed. The argument that there always will be 'high and low', the English rendition of one of his finest and most underrated films, disturbs this director. The title, literally rendered, would be 'Heaven and Hell' expressing Kurosawa's discomfort with the inequities of class.

The kidnapper in *High and Low* (1963) murders a woman purely so that he can test the potency of the drugs he has just purchased. Yet appalled

28   The last shot of *High and Low*: superimposition of the kidnapper and Gondo

as he is by such brutality, Kurosawa does not believe that some should live in mansions high on a hill overlooking the squalor of the working poor, confined to three tatami rooms, freezing in winter, stifling in summer. The class consciousness which pervades Kurosawa's films reflects his youthful attraction to Marxism, which led him to join the Proletarian Artists' League in 1929. He remained active with the movement until 1932 when he suffered a serious illness; class-conscious perception would remain vital to his films.

No matter that Katsushiro was born a samurai, and Shino must forever remain a peasant, they love each other. Kurosawa rejects the conventional notion that their alliance is impossible by having her seduce him. All the while, *Seven Samurai* depicts, with historical accuracy, how inconceivable it was for a samurai to be with the daughter of a farmer.

After Shino and Katsushiro make love, Manzo beats his errant daughter. 'What do you mean, falling for a samurai!' he says to her, and she believes him to be right, even as, wistfully, earlier in the film she confided to Katsushiro, 'I wish I were a samurai's daughter.' Katsushiro had not disputed her nor suggested that it does not matter. 'A farmer's life is wretched,' he agrees. 'You're a samurai and I'm a peasant,' Shino repeats. This barrier can never be put fully out of mind by either of them.

When Kambei and Shichiroji register the identity of the offending samurai, Shichiroji looks over to Katsushiro with an expression of disgust. Yet the next moment, he consoles Manzo with words acknowledging the artificiality of class separation in any humane sense. 'It happens even in a castle,' Shichiroji tells Manzo. The attraction between young men and women overwhelms social convention everywhere and such arbitrary distinctions never fully succeed in keeping people apart.

Even as he mourns the loss of the samurai ethos from Japanese culture and civilisation, Kurosawa ponders whether the rigidity of class distinctions may not have contributed to the demise of this noble class. It is a problem without redress; he allows it to stand without attempting to reconcile the ambiguity. Kikuchiyo is in all respects a samurai, but for birth and class, and the others accept him as such. And if he cannot survive, neither can such authentic samurai as Kyuzo, Gorobei and Heihachi.

Although his focus is on social action, on the fate of societies and classes, Kurosawa is no less concerned with what he identifies in *Something Like an Autobiography* as 'the problem of the self'. It was the theme of his first post-war film, *No Regrets for Our Youth* (1946). Yukie, the woman at the centre of the film, played by Setsuko Hara, undergoes a transformation. She evokes the Japanese woman compliant with the dictates of her culture, occupied with playing the piano and learning flower arranging. She becomes a self-directed person, one who lives by her own hard-won beliefs.

In a classic signature moment of rebellion, Yukie destroys her flower arrangement; Kurosawa offers a shot of the torn blossoms floating in a basin of water. It marks Yukie's passage from a life of self-indulgence, female subservience and inferiority to one of confidence in service to larger ideals. At that transitional moment when Yukie savages her flowers, she becomes a full human being.

Yukie chooses in the end to return to the home of her dead husband's parents, assuming the hard life of a peasant woman in order to contribute to a society in need. 'I felt that without the establishment of the self as a positive value there could be no freedom and no democracy,' Kurosawa said.

'I like unformed characters,' Kurosawa has also confessed. Yukie and Kikuchiyo share this quality. 'It is in watching someone unformed enter the path to perfection that my fascination knows no bounds.' The 'humanism' by which he has defined himself expresses itself in Kurosawa's conviction, conveyed in both films, that especially in periods of historical transition – Japan after the Pacific War, as with Japan in the sixteenth century – people can grow, change and become more vibrant, forceful and ethical than they might otherwise have been.

What attracted Kurosawa instantly to Toshiro Mifune when Kurosawa walked into his audition at the Toho studio was how quickly Mifune could get across an impression, 'the speed of his movements'. In *Seven Samurai*, he develops from being an aimless drifter, alcoholic, alone and roughly aggressive, to becoming a dedicated member of a group with a strong sense of honour. His capacity for selflessness is assumed late in life. He is not, after all, thirteen years old, like the real-life samurai 'Kikuchiyo' whose family papers he has stolen. His new persona is all the more touching for its having been learned.

Hard rain accompanies the final battle between villagers and bandits. It wipes away the illusion that there is moral integrity in the notion of class distinctions. Peasants and samurai alike perish in the driving downpour. As Kurosawa told me, he saw the battle in the rain as obliterating class separation. 'Everybody had to fight for himself. They all melted into the same class.'

Kurosawa as Master Craftsman

There may be no film in the history of cinema which illustrates so completely the power and potential of the medium. Nor is there one which better fulfils Eisenstein's belief that cinema is 'that genuine and ultimate synthesis of all artistic manifestations', embodying a unity of all the arts. Some of the shots, particularly those tableaux of the farmers seated side by side at the inn early in the film, suggest sculpture, 'plastic forms'. In film, as Eisenstein says, placed into motion pictures these studies in form are 'bursting, at long last, ages of immobility'.

The painterly nature of many of Kurosawa's shot compositions, particularly those including groups of samurai, and those of large crowds in deep space, reminiscent of Flemish paintings, reflect Kurosawa's training as a visual artist. The use of crowds, the final battles, illuminate film's special affinity for spectacle.

Hayasaka's music is a high classical interpenetration of motifs. The script of *Seven Samurai* possesses the coherence of literature. It was written by Kurosawa (who as an assistant director was trained in script writing), in collaboration with Shinobu Hashimoto and Hideo Oguni, who together worked with him on his other masterpiece, *Ikiru*, and on *Record of a Living Being* (1955).

As for the medium he finally chose, Kurosawa utilises every technique accessible to the director in this 200-minute film, which took him eighteen months to make. Distributors were uneasy, and in the year it was made *Seven Samurai* was immediately cut by forty minutes and shown in the shortened version both in Japan and abroad. That special effects were not available to him accentuates the power of his film-making.

For the first time, he began to use more than one camera running. Later he would explain that 'it was impossible to predict exactly what would happen in the scene where the bandits attack the peasants' village in a heavy rain storm'. The technique arose out of the exigencies of the filming: there 'was no guarantee that any action could be repeated in exactly the same way twice. So I used three cameras rolling simultaneously.' He would use the same technique in his next film, *Record of a Living Being*, a contemporary drama in which there was virtually no action.

In *Seven Samurai*, he outlined three distinct camera positions: 'A' was the orthodox, what one would expect to take in the action; 'B' was for 'quick, decisive shots'; and 'C' worked 'as a kind of guerrilla unit'. The quantity of footage, of course, was necessary for a work which would embody the very concept of film editing. Nowhere does any later director better fulfil the promise of Eisenstein's innovations in montage than Kurosawa does in this film.

Eisenstein felt certain that with the advent of sound 'only a contrapuntal use of sound in relation to the visual montage piece will afford a new potentiality of montage development and perfection'. In a manifesto he signed with V.I. Pudovkin and G.V. Alexandrov, he declared that 'sound, treated as a new montage element (as a factor divorced from the visual image) will inevitably introduce new means of enormous power to the expression and solution of the most complicated tasks ...'

Eisenstein is worth quoting at length, because Kurosawa, coming of age at the turn of the 1940s, a full decade later, embraced this view entirely. He attributed his conversion to sound used in counterpoint to the image, however, not to Eisenstein, but to the composer Fumio Hayasaka, who worked with him from *Drunken Angel* (1948) through part of *Record of a Living Being*, when Hayasaka died.

For the most part Hayasaka's musical motifs work in *Seven Samurai* to underline the visuals. There are motifs for each main character and for groups of characters. A high-sounding martial music accompanies the samurai; it is used in particular with Kambei, but stands equally for all the samurai. The bandits arrive announced by low-sounding drums, at once ominous and dangerous.

The peasants during their helplessness are greeted by dark choral lamentations. A steady drum-beat, like a heart measuring each beat, creates a special motif for the village elder, the old grandad. The peasants when they are happy, during the harvest and rice planting, are accompanied by a high, lyrical sound, punctuated by drums and flutes. Young love, signalled when Shino and Katsushiro are alone together, offers a sonorous bolero-like sound. The music for Kikuchiyo is upbeat and active, paced to the speed with which this character moves. Throughout, the choral music associated with the peasants is contrasted with a paradoxical triumphant rhythm conveying samurai optimism, confidence and command.

There is even a distinct motif, carried by the bamboo flute, for Rikichi's wife at the fort. It is an eerie sound of anguish expressing her shame and humiliation which prepares the viewer for the horrifying moment when she walks back into the fire, choosing to burn to death rather than face the husband she has disgraced. That she was kidnapped and forced into bondage by bandits would not, in those feudal times, mitigate the disgrace visited upon her husband. Cruelly, she must assume responsibility.

The dark drums of the bandits begin under the Toho logo, as if the threat of their counterparts were present still today, at the moment of the film's viewing. At once Kurosawa suggests the timeliness of oppression, and its universality.

The counterpoint between sound and image becomes all the more pronounced for the otherwise harmonious accompaniment of music to image. As Shino attempts to seduce Katsushiro, the sound of a horse whinnying appears once, and then again. In direct opposition to the lovers' quarrel, it makes the point that at such a conjuncture, in times of war and extremes, matters of love and personal satisfaction must give way to transcendent concerns. Counterpoint is used when Kurosawa can encapsulate out of one moment the meaning of the film as a whole. During episodes of murder and mayhem, birds chirp in the background, as they do in the first scene when the farmers lament their seemingly hopeless fate.

There is astonishingly minimal dialogue in this film. Shino and Katsushiro are allowed a scant ten sentences between them despite several scenes. Dialogue itself, when extended, works in counterpoint through the juxtaposition of words and action. This is the way Kikuchiyo's long monologue on the nature of the farmers, and the responsibility of the samurai for transforming them into 'foxy beasts', works for the film. Kikuchiyo is otherwise inarticulate. The speech gains resonance precisely because samurai rarely express their feelings overtly or convey their thoughts in mere words. It is a function of their identity that action provides the best and clearest manifestation of their feelings, a sensibility and perspective that govern Kurosawa's film style in *Seven Samurai*.

The first shot of the film is a deep long pan over thundering drums. On the horizon are the bandits surveying the village. The bandit group is back lit so that they appear in silhouette, figures of darkness and doom as they dash across the horizon. They will have no names. Only a 'chieftain', a vicious leader with demonic horns protruding from his

The opening shot: bandits backlit against the horizon

armour, as if he were a fugitive from the Teutonic knights of Eisenstein's *Alexander Nevsky*, is even cited individually in the credits. Apart from this, they are a category – 'bandits'.

This first sequence is classic Eisenstein. Kurosawa chooses the cut over the long take at every opportunity. He uses nine shots to draw the viewer down into the village, stopping with a close-up of the backs and rear ends of the women as one enumerates their woes: 'Land tax. Forced Labour. War. Drought. Then the bandits!'

The fragmentation expresses at once the suffering of the peasants, who see no solution to their dilemma short of surrendering everything to the bandits and committing mass suicide. It is as if the duration of peasant suffering were itself endless, their helplessness existing from eternity. That the suffering of farmers has persisted through the ages is conveyed in the later scene in which Kikuchiyo rescues a baby from its mother, who has been speared by the bandits. Somehow summoning the strength she hands her child over. Sinking to his knees in the stream, up to his waist in rushing water, clutching the baby to his chest, Kikuchiyo howls, 'This baby. It's me! The same thing happened to me!'

From the onset, Kurosawa reveals what will be the dominant shot composition of *Seven Samurai*: the situating of men in groups. At moments a shot will contain only samurai, at others, farmers. At times – because in defence of the village class distinctions must be put aside – farmers and samurai occupy the same shot. The fate of one is tied always to the fate of many, and so even when he chooses for distinct emphasis a rare close-up, Kurosawa returns to shots of men in groups.

When in this first sequence Mosuke proposes that they appeal to the magistrate, he is not alone in the shot. Rikichi, burning with anger, a vein bulging in his forehead, forms another sculptural figure. When he leaves the group and turns his back, he begins the action of getting down on his knees, only to complete this motion in the following shot. The match-on-action – a deliberate slowing down of events – will serve in the film as a point of emphasis, what in literature would be conveyed by the rhythm of the sentence, or in words. It is another reflection of Eisenstein's impulse to montage which Kurosawa embraces so thoroughly in this film.

Rikichi's motion is almost a jump-cut, a technique Kurosawa enlists long before its apogee within the films of the French New Wave. In the second shot, Rikichi is closer to the ground than he was when the first shot ended; a piece of the action is absent. The effect is one of discordance which reflects the crisis in the story.

The repetition of shot compositions elucidates the concept of the

'This baby. It's me! The same thing happened to me!'

eternal suffering of the peasants. Just as the crowd of farmers forms a procession as they walk towards the hut of the village patriarch, Gisaku (Kuninori Kodo), affectionately called 'grandad', the same composition will reappear in the town as the people march to observe Kambei's brave action in rescuing a howling baby from a thief who has taken it hostage.

The elder is granted his own visual symbol, the water wheel outside his house, which moves in steady rhythm for the mill. It represents the stability of the village, the permanence of the earth on which peasant life depends no less than grandad's leadership; Kurosawa introduces this symbolic image in three shots in classic Eisensteinian montage, a first, a second, closer, and a third from another angle. The cut takes us inside.

In a rare long take for this film, the grandad – a moving sculpture himself, chiselled out of stone – faces the camera. Every stray hair on his face, every demarcated wrinkle combine to create a work of graphic art, like an etching by Dürer.

After a long silence, he speaks in solemn tones. They must hire samurai, he says. Kurosawa holds the close-up because the advice is at once so outrageous, and daring, and so right. His sculptural approach and fragmentation technique, which defy the demand that the story be kept ever moving forward, urge Kurosawa to offer montages of reaction shots. Rikichi perks up. Manzo reflects his abiding pessimism. 'That's too reckless,' he proclaims, which turns out, for him, to be true. In counterpoint is the drum-beat which also suggests that time is short, emulating the quickening beat of the aged grandad's weary heart. It conveys above all that action must be taken. 'Hire *hungry* samurai,' the grandad adds. He is placed in the centre of the frame for the rare extreme close-up, which adds the director's approval to his words.

Characteristically, Kurosawa's wipe is to a shot in full motion. A samurai walks from right to left of the frame. The heroic musical motif associated with the samurai works here in counterpoint to the images of arrogant, undisciplined samurai whom the desperate villagers solicit hesitantly and at random; one walks by eating pronouncedly, in defiance of samurai etiquette. When the four farmers in town stand outside their inn in search of willing samurai, Kurosawa enlists the telephoto lens to its fullest power.

The space between peasants and wandering *ronin* shrinks, so that they appear so close it is as if they could touch each other, as if they were superimposed. So Kurosawa suggests that in times of such trouble when the social fabric is torn asunder, class differences break down. Kurosawa

36   The magic of the telephoto lens: when the social fabric is torn asunder, class differences break down

has said that he used the telephoto lens because it 'permits the actor to forget the camera more easily', but its effects are much more profound.

At the inn, the shots of the four farmers seated motionless on the platform, in despairing vulnerability, compose a classic sculpture. It is as if they were set in stone, in relief. The Rodin-like shot is broken only by the entrance of the bun-seller with his tray. This painterly aspect emerges in Kurosawa's use of deep space, ironically, deployed by Kurosawa to best advantage within the confines of the inn. The use of deep space forms a counterpoint with Kurosawa's enlistment of the telephoto lens, which collapses the space within the shot, removing the planes between foreground and background. At the same time, Kurosawa often uses a conventional approach to the angle of the camera. He chooses a low angle looking up at the samurai who is so indignant at the suggestion that he defend a village of farmers that in one brutal motion he sends Rikichi sprawling in the dust.

The telephoto lens removing the physical space between farmers and samurai notwithstanding, the farmers appear to have failed. As they make ready to leave, the wind blows up, preparing for the high winds of the latter part of the film. The wind is matched to the extreme high angle Kurosawa uses for an extreme close-up of Rikichi as he pleads passionately with the others not to give up. 'What will you offer them this time?' he demands of Manzo. 'Your daughter?'

As the farmers join the crowd which has discovered something to see, the wind blows hard. There is the sound of the running water of the stream, later to reappear because Rikichi's house in the village, which the samurai will occupy, is on a stream. This reiteration also belies the film's seeming realism.

Kikuchiyo pushes forward to get the best view of Kambei's attack on the kidnapper

Among the many aspects of montage developed by Eisenstein, Kurosawa uses the extension of duration beyond its normal time. He repeats an action as well as a shot, a technique signalling anew that realism is but his surface mode, and it heightens the moment. He extends duration when Kikuchiyo pushes aside the townspeople to get the best view of Kambei's cunning surprise attack on the kidnapper. The action is repeated twice to draw audience attention to Kikuchiyo, the better to establish his later importance in the film. Deep space allows Kurosawa to layer his shots, much in the manner of Mizoguchi, not least in *A Story from Chikamatsu*, a film Mizoguchi made the same year as *Seven Samurai*.

The manipulation of time is at the heart of montage, and Kurosawa's editing reflects this potential. The thief who kidnapped the child emerges from the shack in slow motion, a falling piece of sculpture. The technique is reiterated with the arrogant man whose bravado defies the norm of samurai decorum and who, foolishly, draws a reluctant Kyuzo into a duel he cannot win; in this case his death in slow motion dramatises its opposite: the swiftness of Kyuzo's sword-fighting technique.

The thief dies with his leg outstretched, to Kikuchiyo's delight; it will be the exact position in which Kikuchiyo himself will succumb, as Kurosawa suggests that death is the great equaliser. At the heart of Kurosawa's depiction of action is his orchestration of a virtual ballet, characterised by repetition of shot compositions and sounds, in particular the whinnying of horses, as well as a rich repertoire of recurrent images.

As Kambei leaves, with both Kikuchiyo and Katsushiro following, Kurosawa initiates shot compositions which link the samurai and their common fate. In one shot Kambei stands to the left, as Katsushiro bows to the ground before him; Kikuchiyo stands impatiently at screen right, his sword over his shoulder. With a cut, Katsushiro's bow is revealed to have been so low that he is now excluded from the frame. What remains is a foreshadowing shot of Kambei with Kikuchiyo whom he will later accept as one of them.

The travelling camera is then accompanied by important dialogue, allowing Kambei's first revelations about his life. When the three talk, Kurosawa repositions the camera. He reveals, as he did in the first sequence of the circle of peasants, that he will violate the 180-degree line which decrees that for spectators to maintain a sense of where they are in space, the camera must remain on one side of that line. Kurosawa throughout the film will use the full 360 degrees within which to place one of the three cameras he deploys to generate a sense of life fully depicted in the moment of its unfolding. He even enlists graphics like

The thief, on his tip-toes, falls forward in slow motion ...

... and dies with his leg outstretched

Kikuchiyo dies face down in the mud

maps and charts to orient the viewer to the film space.

A montage between the action and inanimate objects is a favourite technique. The sword Kambei used to dispatch the kidnapper by surprise, its tip bloody, occupies a short take of its own.

Nowhere more elegantly does Kurosawa enlist deep focus for his many layered shots than at the inn where he carves out a foreground, then, characters seated in a background, and further beyond, the street teeming with life where townspeople rush by oblivious to the dilemma of the farmers. This use of deep space allows Kurosawa to elaborate the conflict between motion and motionlessness, and extend the film's avenues of suspense: whether Kambei will accept the offer, whether he will be able to locate six other samurai of equal mind, whether the village will be saved. The image of Kambei's hand holding the bowl of rice up to the peasants presents another such moment. It expresses his humility. Kurosawa endorses Kambei's gesture by closing the scene with a deep fade.

From D.W. Griffith, Sergei Eisenstein and Akira Kurosawa both learned the value to narrative of parallel action. In *Seven Samurai*'s clinic of technique, the director's cutting between two actions simultaneous in time, but at different locations, appears smooth and necessary. Even as the samurai have yet to be gathered, Manzo arrives home with his report. The villagers converge from many directions, another Eisensteinian device, the conflict of motion within the shot, a form of 'potential montage'. The grandad, encompassed by the sound of the water wheel and the drum which signals his fate, admits to his constituents that had he told them to hire ten samurai, they would have brought fifteen. Cutting back to town, Kurosawa enlarges still further his use of deep space, which now reflects how monumental the task will be of finding six more samurai willing to risk their lives for nothing more than food to help such lowly beings as farmers. Class differences, at the same time, are reasserted in the shot compositions emphasising the extraordinariness of the proposition and the improbability of its realisation.

Kambei will occupy the foreground of most of the shots of the samurai. In the early shot where they search the street, Katsushiro is directly behind Kambei, while Rikichi and Yohei, the two remaining villagers, remain in the background. There is full sunlight. Gorobei is granted an extreme close-up to mark the respect to which he is entitled because of his noble character. In the conversations between the samurai, Kurosawa prefers two-shots to the shot reverse shot technique, reflecting their sympathy for each other. That their meeting is monumental is commemorated by the fade.

Yohei sits beside the huge
jar

Drama is also fortified by the repeated match-on-action. At the inn, Kurosawa uses it as Yohei sinks to the floor in shame after the rice, which he has been entrusted to guard, is found to have disappeared. Through the use of the telephoto lens, the jar which once held the stolen rice, becomes so large that it dwarfs Yohei, overwhelming him. The object has greater import here than the people as a shot contains no more than Yohei's hands retrieving, grain by grain, the few scattered bits of rice remaining behind. The coins which Katsushiro rains down upon the rice grains are an application of Eisenstein's synaesthesia, the substitution of the part for the whole. The concept is that, young as he is, Katsushiro embodies samurai generosity.

To heighten the moment, Kurosawa bleeds the shot of sound, in homage to another of Eisenstein's montage techniques, the conflict

A hand holds out a bowl of rice: Kambei's moral elegance

Coins among rice grains

between sound and silence. Kurosawa had enlisted this technique most remarkably in *Ikiru* when Watanabe (Takashi Shimura) goes out into the street and steps off the curb into heavy traffic only for the shot to be accompanied by absolute silence. Having just been told he has stomach cancer, and been presented with a verdict of death, Watanabe is lost in his thoughts; as he is nearly run over, as he comes to himself, suddenly the roar of traffic overwhelms the shot.

By the time Gorobei walks into the street to look for Heihachi, Kurosawa has prepared for the deep space which now enlarges the life of the town in yet more layers – a man with a horse, mothers with children and bustling people going on with their lives. With Kambei and Gorobei, and Kambei paired with Shichiroji, Kurosawa includes both Gorobei and Heihachi in the shot.

This elaboration of the film's central theme is also conveyed in the content of their conversation, one which reveals a harmony between the samurai that will persist throughout the film. There is never a harsh word spoken between any of them. Kambei will chastise only Kikuchiyo and that because he is, after all, only an aspiring samurai, and must learn how to be one. Among the others there is congeniality. Heihachi in his first scene confides in modest and ironic self-deprecation that in matters of battle, he runs away. 'A splendid principle!' Gorobei agrees. In such moments of affirmation the basis of the Japanese preference for consensus is confirmed.

Kurosawa, however, makes it clear that not all samurai behave so nobly. Kyuzo is forced into a duel with a man whom he knows is hopelessly outmatched and whom he will kill. He stands as still as sculpture. By now Kurosawa can easily make use of the 360 degrees of

Kyuzo stands, as still as sculpture, facing his challenger

Five samurai and Yohei are present as Kikuchiyo rolls out the scroll

On the way to the village:
the samurai sit above on a
cliff as Kikuchiyo catches a
fish with his bare hands

space for his cameras. This scene of foolish bravado and false pride gives way to the last scenes at the inn where the samurai are depicted in group shots. In another match-on-action Kambei stands to greet Kyuzo, who has stood listening to Kambei's account of his life.

The group is divided with the return of a now very drunk Kikuchiyo. In a close shot Kambei's expression alters as he recognises this young man; Shichiroji and Heihachi are pictured behind him in the shot. Reactions to events will be group reactions. Five samurai and Yohei are present in the shot where Kikuchiyo rolls out the scroll which 'proves' that he's a samurai. Later all six samurai and the two farmers will sit at the top of a cliff eating while below Kikuchiyo catches a fish with his bare hands, emphasising his peasant origins.

As the samurai begin their journey to the village, the two peasants walk together; the samurai in a full group follow behind. Kurosawa cuts one last time to events back in the village where the peasants, and in particular Manzo, face with trepidation the arrival of dangerous warriors in their village. It is in this scene that Manzo forcibly cuts short the hair of his daughter Shino so that she will not fall prey to these samurai.

The fast pan accompanies the chase of father and daughter. The chase – that most cinematic of devices according to Siegfried Kracauer in his *Theory of Film* – is a potent film element and works well in a film in which there is, as Richie says, so much movement. Kracauer notes that the need for motion, the *sine qua non* of cinema, led Griffith to include a 'chase pure and simple', a 'last-minute rescue' at the endings of his films. The chases in *Seven Samurai* are many, but each carries a particular

Manzo forcibly cuts
Shino's hair

significance. Heihachi chases Kikuchiyo within the confined space of the inn. Kambei chases Mosuke when he and a group of followers separate themselves. The bandits chase Kikuchiyo who has wandered into their lair. The final battles involve one chase after another. The intensity of motion matches the urgency of the farmers' situation.

When the samurai are met in the village with silence, the villagers in hiding, Kurosawa once more expresses the ensuing confusion by violating the 180-degree line so that the sense of space becomes ambiguous. All six are in the frame, treated alike in this shocking violation of hospitality.

Each montage technique reiterates the central theme. When the alarm is sounded, the samurai race from the grandad's house, where they have been pondering the fact that the peasants will not even emerge to greet them, to the heart of the village. Instead of using one shot, here Kurosawa enlists six, all graphic matches, each identical and displaying one of the six samurai running from left to right at the centre of the shot. Each runs at top speed, his commitment total and unquestioning. Only Kikuchiyo, who has not yet been accepted as a samurai, is missing. This graphic match is particularly startling because of its contrast by this moment in the film with the many shot compositions depicting men in groups. The peasants emerge from all directions in motion as Kikuchiyo sounds the village alarm in front of the same bridge where he will meet his death.

Shot composition, whether of people or of objects, furthers the narrative and foreshadows events. The map appears only with the addition of pointing fingers, like the composition of Yohei's hands gathering rice. A pattern emerges of Kambei, Gorobei and Katsushiro walking through the village, entering shots where the others are training villagers, and then exiting at screen right. Kyuzo instructs his group with spears; Heihachi offers a pep talk about bandits being afraid no less than they; Kikuchiyo trains his group with broad jokes. Intersecting are tableaux-like shots of Kambei, Gorobei and Katsushiro surveying the village for purposes of military strategy. Such stylised sequences in themselves transcend the narrow category of realism.

The first scene between Katsushiro and Shino follows. In an ironic reprise of the moment of the rape in *Rashomon*, Kurosawa has Katsushiro first lie down in the field of flowers, the music bolero-like, the camera panning an idyllic sunlit sky with almost a full 360-degree circle. The scene is punctuated with Katsushiro seated facing right in the field of flowers while Shino sits, embarrassed, facing the camera. Later, just prior to the arrival of the three scouts, they are in the identical location, but side by side facing the same direction, their rapport having been achieved.

When Kikuchiyo chastises the samurai for their historical abusive treatment of farmers, the others are revealed together in the shot. Only Kikuchiyo, the outsider, remains apart. The angle is high, looking down on the samurai, as their helplessness and vulnerability in battle is revealed. Thus does Kurosawa reiterate the central paradox of the film. As powerful as it has been, the samurai class is now vulnerable. It has lost direction and purpose, and samurai are steadily dying off. The huge collection of

Katsushiro and Shino sit awkwardly apart ... but later a rapport is achieved, which is reflected in the new shot composition

swords confiscated from dead samurai belongs, after all, to the villagers.

Conveying the pain felt by Kurosawa himself, this is a moment of pathos in which sound is all but obliterated; you hear only the running water of the stream and Heihachi's striking the ground compulsively with a small stick. The silence is broken by Kikuchiyo's loud tirade: 'What do you think of farmers? They pose as saints but are full of lies!' He flings a suit of armour scavenged from a fallen samurai, and concealed by the villagers, into the water. The samurai remain silent, stunned and motionless. At the barn where Kikuchiyo later takes refuge with Rikichi, there will be a corresponding silence, broken only by the sound of an owl and the musical theme associated with Kikuchiyo.

The fade-in now is not to sun, but to rain. Five samurai are in the shot as Heihachi explains the symbolism of the flag he has sewn. Part of the realism which subsists within the stylised moments involves weather, and there is rain as often as there is sunlight and bright skies.

Kyuzo practises in the rain. He spies Katsushiro and Shino under a diagonal set of tree trunks, the conflict within the shot presaging their final separation. Shino gives the rice which Katsushiro has saved for her to Kyuemon's granny, because her son was killed by the bandits.

Another aspect of the film's realism is that Kurosawa includes people of all ages, groups of children, young couples, the middle-aged and the very old. In counterpoint to the pity felt by everyone else is Kikuchiyo's anger. 'I hate all wretched people,' he declares, so covering his own sorrow. 'I feel disgusted with them. I want to do something.' He speaks here, quite obviously, for director Kurosawa.

The reversion to order marks the close of the first half of the film. Kambei holds a baby and is composed in a shot containing only Gorobei and many villagers. Outside, the camera circles, rising to a high angle in preparation for Mosuke's rebellion and Kambei's articulation of the central theme of the film. Dust and earth blow to signal the fade and the musical intermission, which methodically reiterates each of the sequential motifs.

Kurosawa reopens the film with a comic scene centring on Kikuchiyo's amazement during the harvest that there are so many women in the village. Extreme close-ups take advantage of Mifune's expressiveness. Deep space dramatises: Shino works in the field; Manzo rises up out of the waving wheat to watch her; suddenly Shichiroji appears, as if magically, between them, creating another spatial plane. The growing alienation of father and daughter is expressed within the composition of this single shot.

Harvest opens the second
half of the film: suddenly
Shichiroji appears, as if
magically, between Manzo
and Shino, creating
another spatial plane

Kyuzo, buried to the waist in flowers, completely still

The exigencies of communication unfold as well as Heihachi attempts to persuade Rikichi to unburden himself of the pain he has endured since his wife was kidnapped. The long take produces no result. 'I've nothing bottled up,' Rikichi lies.

The intensification of counterpoint foreshadows the final battles. The sounds of bolero which accompany the following scene between Shino and Katsushiro are interrupted by signature whinnying of the scouts' horses. A tilt down as Katsushiro runs to look, reveals to the spectator the ominous presence of the horses, and the bandit music now grows louder. Six samurai run in tandem, calling softly to each other 'they must not see us'.

When Kyuzo and Kikuchiyo are sent to the woods to ambush the bandit scouts, the tilt is used more as it takes us up into a tree to observe Kikuchiyo moving now like a panther or a leopard. To his left, in the same shot, we observe Kyuzo below, buried to the waist in flowers, completely still. Katsushiro, however, trembles involuntarily, unable to keep still, and the flowers around him shudder. These same flowers had begun to move when Katsushiro first heard the horses and realised that the bandits had come. Movement alternates with stillness. The encounter itself is brief; it is punctuated by a fast wipe to a close-up of the prisoner straining at his ropes. The telephoto lens encapsulates the unity of the erupting crowd bent on revenge.

As the battles with the bandits progress, Kurosawa places his characters in motion, and his camera moves with them. The travelling shot was his signature and it is provided full expression in the ride to the bandits' fort. The deep tilt is used more frequently in the film's second half, nowhere more dramatically than in the scene of this ride.

At the bandits' fort,
stylisation conflicts with
realism

The tilt downward begins, continuing as the samurai ride by on a
road, and makes its way down. A wipe halts the motion, only for the
camera to enter the frame left under the waterfall. This downward motion,
the most sweeping and elaborate tilt in all of Kurosawa's cinema, reflects
the tragic outcome to follow: the death of Heihachi during this raid.

The raid itself is highly stylised. The three samurai – Kyuzo,
Heihachi and Kikuchiyo – stand side by side in profile, peering inside –

Wide angle stasis: samurai and peasants mourn Heihachi

another pictorial moment. The parallelism reflects, once more, that they are equal in value and commitment. A montage of shots from within the hut depicts the bandits and their women through images of dangling arms and legs, part substituting for the whole.

The samurai set fire to the hideout. When the bandits emerge, reacting to the smoke, a montage of sounds returns the film to realism: there is a mixture of shouts, flames crackling, horses neighing and water running with splashes as the bandits fling themselves into the running stream where Heihachi will meet his fate.

That long tilt at the start of the sequence also reiterated the ellipsis of time which Kurosawa requires in this film. The collapse of real time began with the samurai walk from the town to the village, and is elaborated now in the funeral of Heihachi. There is again a high wind and blowing dust. In contrast to the chaotic movement of the raid, we now experience stasis, as samurai above and peasants below mourn Heihachi. In a dramatic break with the motionlessness of the scene, Kikuchiyo plunges Heihachi's sword into his grave.

Kambei and Gorobei occupy a shot together, their friendship having deepened. 'We were counting on him to cheer us when the situation became gloomy,' Kambei laments. With this pause, the sentiment is broken by Kikuchiyo's frantic run as he races to the house, grabs the flag and climbs up onto another house to plant it on the roof. In a long shot, all turn to watch. The flag, like the map before it, and the chart of circles connoting the bandits to come, blows in the wind to the sound of a saluting trumpet. A shot of the group, now ready to fight, gives way to a second shot of the flag. A shot of women, as much a part

Close-up of the banner, punctuating Heihachi's funeral

of the battle as the men, is replaced once again by one of the banner. This time the camera tilts downward to reveal all its symbols – samurai, Kikuchiyo with his own personal triangular symbol and the farmers.

Kurosawa cuts to two more shots of the peasants only to return to the banner-flag for a final tilt. Kikuchiyo now looks up and in an eye-line match on the horizon the bandits – again backlit, again in silhouette – ride into the shot, as if by magic, sent from hell. The moment is operatic and points to the climactic scenes to come. Time, after having been slowed, is now accelerated. In a short take, only the grandad can be seen at the site of the graves. In four shots everyone runs to his post while Kurosawa adds two pans, one left to right, the other right to left, as the bandits, confounded by the fence, find themselves unable to enter the village.

The battles themselves – which Kurosawa renders exciting through the use of the telephoto lens, enabling his camera to appear to get down beneath the horses' hooves – are characterised by the cut. From this point on, Kurosawa rarely slows down. One moment when he does is the dissolve between Kyuzo, nodding off to sleep, and a shot of horses' hooves returning to the furore of the action. Apart from this moment, the wipe is Kurosawa's signature optical transition between shots. It allows him to maintain the swift pace of the narrative. At moments when the village needs to pause, he enlists the deep fade.

The *mise en scène* will be devoted from here onward to the reiteration of motifs already established. The water wheel reappears, but this time there are two shots of the old grandad, his back to the camera. Even as the samurai must not leave their posts, the old patriarch refuses to depart from his house. Amid the tumult, he sits motionless, as if reconciled to his death in a resignation Kurosawa reveals but does not further explore.

The old man's refusal to leave his burning shack, however, brings the young couple, who are his relatives, protectively back to his side and thus ensures their death. With the water wheel now on fire, emblematic of the old man's demise, which goes unseen, the woman emerges with her baby in her arms. Kikuchiyo rushes to the rescue. He grabs the baby from the dying woman and sinks to his knees in the stream. The scene ends with two shots, one of the water wheel on fire, the other with the wheel out of place, broken and now only partially on fire, the mill destroyed.

Kikuchiyo's animal instincts, his sense of smell, as he sniffs out bandits hiding in the water, becomes a samurai trait. Shichiroji's keen senses will ensure his survival. 'I smell a gun fuse!' he says as he orders his men down, a seemingly unimportant moment. Yohei in another tableau stands motionless, his mouth wide open in a grotesque expression of dismay. He holds the end of his spear; the other end is placed firmly in the heart of a bandit. As the two cultures are contrasted once more, Kikuchiyo releases the spear and the bandit falls dead. Peasants become warriors, but it requires a huge distortion of their characters.

Kambei's chart, counting and marking off the dead bandits, serves also as graphic foreshortening. It informs the spectator that the war will not be endless. It grants specific meaning to Kyuzo's words as he returns from bandit territory having secured one of the three guns: 'killed two'.

Kurosawa has offered a montage of those awaiting his return. A peasant group is pictured as restless and ridden with anxiety while the hours stretch on. The samurai, half asleep, are equally uneasy. Out of the fog and mist the figure of Kyuzo emerges in extreme long shot as if he were a ghost in a visual foreshadowing of his death.

Kambei examines the gun as if it were some foreign object, which, in fact, it is. He will not use it, and he will win the war, whatever it costs, without the technology that has become the direct enemy of his entire way of life. The gun represents an era, a historical time in which he will become atavistic and no longer have a place.

It is in extreme close-up that Katsushiro tells Kyuzo, 'you're great'. His action is in marked contrast to Shino's appeal a moment earlier to Katsushiro to make love to her, even as she proclaims that she is not concerned about the future. The moment is conveyed in shallow focus, reflecting the director's allocation of lesser value to personal desire.

For the battles, Kurosawa experiments with the telephoto lens. Horses' hooves move in the mud, all but splattering it in the face of the spectator. A graphic match of two shots brings the two armour-clad bandit leaders directly into the village. These matches, unlike the earlier six graphic matches of the samurai, are the discordant right to left. A bandit crawls as if under the horses' hooves, courtesy of the telephoto lens.

This evocative discordance is reiterated in all the final episodes. When Kikuchiyo decides to leave his post to emulate Kyuzo, and earn the same praise, by capturing another of the guns, he is shot in high angle looking down, an expression of Kurosawa's disapproval, later to be rendered in words by Kambei. A diagonal tilt as he races into the woods underlines the point. The travelling camera winds up behind him as he is seated by the side of the bandit with the gun whose fuse Kikuchiyo had sniffed in the wind. Unlike Kyuzo, whose return was accompanied by calm, Kikuchiyo brings bandits chasing him on foot to the edge of the village. In the next moment the rest of the gang rides in.

Shichiroji sleeps with his
hands folded on his spear

On the night before the culminating battle, Kurosawa, for the last time, plays upon the conflict between stasis and motion. Shichiroji sleeps with his hands folded on his spear, alert even while he is semi-conscious. Unlike Kikuchiyo, who snores, Kyuzo and Shichiroji sleep as if their eyes are open. Sake emerges, and fancy food, validating Kikuchiyo's earlier speech about how 'foxy' peasants are. Everyone rests for the final test to come. Shichiroji, however, says he will keep watch.

Kikuchiyo remains at the graves. Of all the samurai he feels things most deeply, and Kambei rubs his head in homage to that devotion. He brings Kikuchiyo the jug of sake, as the camera looks down on them, foreshadowing imminent death.

A raging bonfire bisects the shot with Katsushiro on one side of the fire, symbolising their passion, and Shino on the other. When they come

A bonfire symbolises the
passion of Shino and
Katsushiro

together, the fire is now in the background of the shot, and when they make love the flickering shadows caused by the fire mingle with the patterns on their costumes. At such moments, Kurosawa the painter merges with Kurosawa the film director.

Once the lovemaking ends, the choral musical motif denoting peasant suffering takes over. Manzo awaits them and the joys of young love give way to their consequences. Kambei rubs his head once more when he learns that the woman is Shino, the name Katsushiro has whispered in his sleep. Katsushiro himself standing, his head hanging, is shown in relief, while Shino, knowing that they can never be together, continues to lie on the ground sobbing, even as it begins to rain.

This long sequence ends with shots not of the people, but of the fire. The rain causes the fire to die down, and it is this rain which forms the transition to the final day of battle.

The bars represent the imprisonment of all *ronin* in their fate

Many marvellous moments of cinematic art occur in the final climactic scenes. Among them is a semi-match-on-action. Kambei picks up his bow and places the arrow. There is an intervening shot of the bandit chieftain riding by, only in the next shot for Kambei to follow through and release the arrow. In true Eisensteinian fashion, Kurosawa has Kambei shoot the arrow in one shot, only to have it strike home in another, suggesting the more defiant moment on the Odessa steps where Eisenstein has a shot fired only to cut to a woman already wounded, with the spectator experiencing the moment of impact without having actually viewed it.

The visual of a house with slats, which began at the inn, comes to its fruition now as the bandit leaders hide behind bars in just such a house.

Mortally wounded, Kyuzo flings his sword, symbol of his soul, in defiance

These bars reflect the imprisonment of all *ronin* in their fate; the six heroic men whom we have followed and the bandits who have chosen a different course. It is through these bars that both Kyuzo and Kikuchiyo are fired upon and killed.

By the end, the shot compositions so merge samurai and peasants that Kyuzo is barely distinguishable. He is one among many in a group of fighters as the shot which will kill him rings out. Mortally wounded, he flings his sword, symbol of his soul, to the heavens in a final gesture of samurai defiance.

That Kikuchiyo is less wise in the ways of war allows him impetuously to approach the house where the chieftain is holding the women as hostages, despite his having been warned. His courage outweighs his bravado as, having been shot, he nevertheless manages to make his way inside and kill the bandit leader. The chieftain meets his end holding in his hands the last of the three guns possessed by the bandits. He is unable to use it, Kurosawa's protest against the coming world ruled by technology.

The flag in the rain and the horses occupy the last shot of the film proper, just before its philosophical coda. All the people have vanished.

The flag in the rain

In every shot, over every cut, Kurosawa has expressed the essential conflict of his film, that between the value of the samurai culture and its coming obsolescence.

His later work will be coloured by a nostalgia for the lost values he praises in *Seven Samurai*, including even *Dersu Uzala* (1975), set and filmed in Russia. 'The power of his personality', Kurosawa wrote in reference to a Chinese character named Chen Pao in the script of that film, 'is evidently the result of his intelligence, self-control, and ability to make others obey his orders.' He could have been describing Kambei.

Kurosawa and Japanese Film; Kurosawa and his Critics

He was at war with the critics, beginning in the late 1930s when he worked as an assistant director. He disliked them in particular for seeing in his films ideas that were not his own. 'The things they say they see are so far off the beam', he wrote finally, 'that you would think they were possessed by some kind of demon.' Only samurai resignation calms him down. 'I suppose nothing can be done about critics.'

The critics upset him throughout his career, in particular in their attempts to elucidate his intentions. 'They try to nail down every scene with an explanation,' he told me. 'I object to this practice. The film is a whole entity. I don't know myself what my message is within a particular sequence. There are scenes which I play down ... in which I conceal my real view.'

As for *Seven Samurai*, he said, 'sometimes my peasants act silly, being real peasants. Sometimes they may act like warriors, but this is not 'my real concept in that film.' Worst of all, he felt, the Japanese critics had put him in a single category and dismissed his films in that way. He was a 'Western' director, he appealed to Western audiences. Just as, he explained, the intentions of the samurai with respect to helping the peasants were 'mixed', so his own films were 'much more nuanced and complex' than the critics had allowed that they were.

As Donald Richie has pointed out, *Seven Samurai* was attacked by Japanese critics even before it was released, an experience remarkably similar to that of Oliver Stone with *JFK* (1991). He was told that he was 'wasting time', and that he was spending too much money. When the film finally appeared, Kurosawa issued a manifesto, explaining that the *jidai-geki* was at an impasse, implying that with *Seven Samurai* he had rescued the genre.

As his career developed, Kurosawa would face not only the absurdities of critics, but the disparagement of the generation of directors which came after him. These men rebelled crudely against his artistic authority, counterposing their avant-garde impulse to his historical interests. Their lack of respect for those who came before may be contrasted with the way Kurosawa himself paid homage to a wide variety of directors he revered as teachers. These included not only Yamamoto, whom Kurosawa called, affectionately, 'Yama-san', but multiple others. In his *Autobiography*, he names Yasujiro Shimazi, Sadao Yamanaka, who worked in the *jidai-geki* as well, and Kenji Mizoguchi, whom he acknowledged as the greatest of Japanese directors. He cites Yasujiro Ozu – who defended him against the wartime censors, and whose films are so unlike his own – and Mikio Naruse, with whom he worked as an assistant on one film, *Avalanche* (1938), a film since lost.

It would not be so for Masahiro Shinoda and Nagisa Oshima, both of whom felt that their cinematic voices could not be heard unless they distanced themselves from Kurosawa – his style, his themes and especially his wide international reputation. I met them both during a trip to Japan in 1972, when I also spoke at length with Kurosawa. 'Kurosawa has exhausted himself pursuing the travelling camera,' Shinoda quipped. To Shinoda, he represented no more than a 'simplistic humanism', one which had long outlived its time. It was as if younger painters had to challenge Velasquez or Rembrandt, or Beckett felt it necessary to dismiss Shakespeare, and Joyce belittled Fielding in order to explore new means of perception and locate innovations reflective of their own times.

Shinoda did admit that Kurosawa was resented by younger directors in part because 'he had the advantage of large sums of money to spend on his films and they did not'. In fact, by 1972, Kurosawa was finding it difficult to attract that money. As Masaki Kobayashi, whose *jidai-geki*, such as *Harakiri* (1962), reveal the marked influence of Kurosawa, told me, 'the movies which Kurosawa-san is interested in are so expensive to produce that none of the five major companies is, at present, willing to undertake the production'.

Shinoda himself has worked in the genre of the *jidai-geki*, and his *Assassination* (1964) which chronicles the tumultuous last days of the Tokugawa dynasty – notably the plots and conspiracies of the *bakumatsu*, the last days of the shogunate – reflects many influences of Kurosawa. Borrowing from Kurosawa, Shinoda situates his story during one of the deepest moments of transition in Japanese history, although he does not admit to the obvious impact Kurosawa had on such a choice.

Oshima, who, unlike Shinoda, eschewed the period film, reacted violently to my mere mention of Kurosawa. Asking him to respond to the work of this director was nothing short of apostasy. He scoffed at what he termed Kurosawa's 'so-called artistic films', implying that their presumptive 'realism' precluded his taking them seriously. For Oshima, Kurosawa drew so heavily on Japanese tradition as inevitably to force his audience into complacency. 'Our generation cannot rely on the congeniality of our all being Japanese in order to communicate,' he argued. That Kurosawa had brought Japanese film to a Western audience meant that he must be pandering to Western values and politics. Shuji Terayama, apparently more charitable, told me that when he was a young man of twenty-four he liked the work of Kurosawa very much. Later he too rejected it, claiming he felt pity when he saw *Dodes'ka-den* (1970). 'Oshima and Shinoda say they hate Kurosawa,' he noted. 'But I don't hate Kurosawa.' At the same time Terayama felt that Kurosawa's adherence to the structure of the classic Hollywood film meant that for a director like himself, Kurosawa could not be meaningful. Of this generation which immediately followed Kurosawa's, only Shohei Imamura felt secure enough to define his work without the need to diminish Kurosawa's art. Of this group of directors, it is, paradoxically, Imamura's films which have best endured.

Through style and his philosophy, if not by attacking those who came before, Kurosawa at once distinguished himself from his own predecessors, forging a cinematic identity very different from theirs. Editing Yamamoto's *Horses* (1941), he was criticised by his mentor for sacrificing drama to *mono-no-aware*. This is Ozu's prevailing emotion, that sweet sense of the passing moment, the transitoriness of all things

'Isn't life disappointing?'
Kyoko and Noriko in the
final sequence of *Tokyo
Story*

The final shot of *Tokyo
Story*: boats on the river
supplant human beings

which forms the culminating moment of *Tokyo Story* (1953). 'Isn't life disappointing?' the youngest daughter of the family, Kyoko, declares. She is brought to her senses by her sister-in-law, Noriko, played by Setsuko Hara, whose husband has died in the war. 'Yes, it is,' she smiles with that peace that passeth understanding, the reflection of a transcendence paramount in the film art of Ozu.

Disturbed by the world's injustice, furious at the perpetual cycle of human misery, Kurosawa is incapable of closing a film on such an emotion. Even if he embraced his father's belief in the educational value of cinema, and sought to make the world better, and people less selfish, although he devised no complete solution, resignation and acceptance were never options for him.

His rebellion centred on the exposure of the pain, and in how social configurations, in particular, class differences, engender and exacerbate suffering. His films imply the need for a permanent resistance to the cruelty of society, a renewed and ever-renewing struggle against the injustices of each succeeding status quo.

In *Seven Samurai* historical accuracy and attention to detail are matched by the subjectivity of the film-maker, a set of values which Kurosawa attaches to history; *Seven Samurai* is a work of fiction, not, finally, one of history, and Kurosawa's accomplishment lies in his seamless blending of the social forces and the facts, of an epoch with his own interpretation of their meaning over time.

To express his very personal perspective, Kurosawa immersed himself in a strong dramatic style which embodies Eisenstein's view that film and conflict were synonymous. In the process, he revolutionised Japanese film. Kurosawa defined traditional Japanese resignation as diminishing and suffocating, an aesthetic divorce from the passion for change. As Donald Richie notes, he contrasted earlier films, so unlike his own, as '*assari shite iru* [light, plain, wholesome], like *ochazuke*', green tea over rice, the title of one of Ozu's films, *The Flavour of Green Tea Over Rice* (1952). He was not, he declared, like Ozu, willing to renounce conflict and a struggle to make the world better in favour of the easy tranquillities of *mono-no-aware*. *Seven Samurai*, he hoped when he set out to make that film, would be 'a film which was entertaining enough to eat', a film with a richness hitherto unknown. He was not like Ozu and he was not like Mizoguchi, his master in artistry, and the director for whom he felt 'the greatest admiration'. What Kurosawa appreciated most about Mizoguchi was that he was 'the first Japanese director to demand authentic sets and props', a credo he would adopt for his own *mise en scène*.

It led to the endless polishing of floor boards in *Seven Samurai*, which added to them the patina of centuries, and the staining of the fabric for the costumes; it led to the stained tea cups in *Red Beard* (1965), his last great *jidai-geki*. Mizoguchi portrayed women and merchants; Kurosawa enjoyed most depicting samurai. 'I think I am best at delineating *bushi*,' he said commemorating Mizoguchi as Japanese film's 'truest creator' at the time of that director's death.

Kurosawa separated himself from the greatest of his predecessors – Ozu, Mizoguchi and Naruse – in one other respect. Despite the brilliance of his portrayal of the character Yukie in *No Regrets for Our Youth*, the women in his films are rarely fully developed characters, capable of the growth and moral evolution of the men. From the wife in *Rashomon* to her counterpart in *High and Low*, the women in his later films are flat.

After the Pacific War, the office of General MacArthur set forth a series of themes which Japanese film directors were prohibited from addressing. Among these were 'approval of the oppression or degradation of wives'. Rather, films were to focus on, among other themes, 'how every human being and every class of society was respected'. To make *Utamaro and His Five Women* (1946), Joseph L. Anderson and Donald Richie point out, Mizoguchi had to promise the censors at SCAP that he would also make a modern film about female emancipation. Kurosawa's Yukie is born of this historical moment in Japanese film.

Shino in *Seven Samurai*, the only female character in the film with a name, is a one-dimensional character. She is the stereotype of the farm girl: a peasant whose impulses are physical, whose existence is grounded in the cycles of farm life and whose responses throughout the film are predictable. Her hair is cut because her father fears she will be seduced; her sexual drive leads her to taunt Katsushiro into having sexual intercourse with her: 'You ... you're not a real samurai. Not a *real* samurai,' she sobs, frustrated by his reluctance to consummate their relationship. Perhaps after Yukie, Kurosawa could find no equally powerful story of a woman's struggle.

Despite its perfection as a work of art, *Seven Samurai* has been the least written about and the most misunderstood of Kurosawa's films, both in Japan and abroad. In the West among contemporary critics, the infatuation with 'theory', and the aversion to history with its scepticism regarding objective truth, has led younger critics to pretend that Kurosawa's masterpiece is in fact one of his lesser works.

If the 'real world' is itself a questionable prospect, not only morality but discourse itself is relative, not at all the thrust of Kurosawa's approach. If history is, in essence, irrelevant, to art as to humane experience, what then was one to make of Kurosawa in general and *Seven Samurai* in particular with its depiction of how the fate of individuals is wrought only through a struggle with history? Many critics choose simply to ignore the film. A recent academic study, James Goodwin's *Akira Kurosawa and Intertextual Cinema*, scarcely mentions *Seven Samurai*. In his post-structuralist *Kurosawa*, Mitsuhiro Yoshimoto, in a forty-page chapter entitled 'Seven Samurai', devotes a scant seven pages to the film itself.

In the two essays about Kurosawa in his *Currents in Japanese Cinema*, 'The Meaning of Life in Kurosawa's Films' and 'Kurosawa's Fathers', even Japanese critic, Tadao Sato, who belongs to an earlier left-wing tendency, offers not a single sentence about *Seven Samurai*. In his chapter on Kurosawa's development, Noël Burch offers one single dismissive footnote to *Seven Samurai*, labelling it 'the finest of

Kurosawa's minor *jidai-geki*'. His reason for dismissing the film is remarkably similar to Shinoda's charge that Kurosawa is guilty of 'simplistic humanism'. Burch's explanation comes in a discussion of *High and Low*: 'Faithful to the ideology that had dominated Kurosawa's films since the very start, this one tells us that "there is much misery among us but our police force is excellent" and that "a chauffeur may earn less than a capitalist but class difference can succumb to good will and human solidarity".' That Kurosawa has not depicted here the rebellion of the oppressed marks him as 'simplistic', and is enough to discount *Seven Samurai* for Burch, no matter that the film is unique in its depiction of the injustices of class society. A similar distress with Kurosawa appears in Richard Tucker's disagreement with Donald Richie on whether Kurosawa is indeed 'the greatest humanist of the Japanese cinema'. Tucker dissents. 'There are other film-makers who have a clearer regard for the individual in Japanese society, the individual free from the constraints of a feudal relationship,' he writes. The directors he has in mind are Kon Ichikawa and Masaki Kobayashi.

In Japan, a pseudo-Marxist view has approached the film from a similar premise, distorting Kurosawa's perspective. A Kyoto symposium in which I took part in 1972 was infused with a general dislike of Kurosawa by the Japanese critics and Japanese director Nagisa Oshima, who also participated. (I had been invited to Japan by the *Mainichi Shimbun* newspaper as the sole American winner of an essay contest on the subject of how foreigners view Japanese culture.) Critic Michitaro Tada argued that since everything is seen in a specific social situation in *Seven Samurai*, it followed that 'there is no psychological conflict'. Oshima echoed this view, complaining that the collective fight was not deepened into individual struggle. Worse, he objected to the unfashionable presence in *Seven Samurai* and in other of Kurosawa's films of what he called a 'superman struggle', and the presence of the leader, the figure larger than life whose wisdom and superiority cause him to dwarf all other characters. What is astonishing here is the willed denial of Kurosawa's treatment of transformation – among farmers and samurai. 'In my films', Shinoda told me, 'I have tried to show the present through the past and history, coming around to the truth that all Japanese culture flows from imperialism and the emperor system.' Oshima agreed. Kurosawa's 'elitism' seemed offensive and retrograde.

What is good about the samurai, Tada thought, was that through civil disorder they were forced to 'give up some of their tradition'. What he admired in Kurosawa's depiction, no matter that it bears no relation to the film, is that 'they are now free as human beings to reject tradition'. His example was the early scene in which, disguising himself as a priest to rescue the baby, Kambei cuts off his topknot. That Kurosawa was expressing through these six, not a rejection of samurai tradition, but its ideal expression, did not occur to him.

In the angriest of the charges against Kurosawa, Tadao Sato and Tada accused Kurosawa of a 'condescending' attitude towards the peasantry in *Seven Samurai*. He had portrayed his farmers as weak and stupid, they complained, for which he could not be forgiven. Because they are incapable of defending themselves, because they enlist a superior class on their behalf, Kurosawa is simultaneously renouncing belief that the oppressed have the capacity to overthrow those who oppress them.

Pointedly, Sato listed as the peak of Kurosawa's work *Record of a Living Being*, the film he made right after *Seven Samurai*, about a man so obsessed by the possibility of another atomic bomb being dropped on Japan that he insists on moving his entire family to Brazil. He admired *Ikiru*, *Yojimbo* and *High and Low* as well because they 'most challenge Western culture', even as Kurosawa's supposed superficiality emerges in his admiration of detective Tokura in *High and Low* and the paltriness, the unsatisfactoriness of the theme that all we can do in a society of injustice and disorder is 'continue the effort'. *Seven Samurai* was not worthy even of mention, except in the wrongheadedness, for Sato, of Kurosawa's view that 'only a handful of people are great'. 'This is wrong,' Sato said. 'There is too great a gap between the central figure and the others. Worst of all, the farmers are too stupid.'

When I told him about this discussion, Kurosawa defended himself: 'I wanted to say that after everything the peasants were the stronger, closely clinging to the earth. It is the samurai who were weak because they were being blown by the winds of time.' Kurosawa was, however, being somewhat disingenuous. The peasants are strong not because they are admirable or beautiful or possess any enviable qualities, but because of their brute energy, determination and persistence. They are strong as well because of their usefulness as providers of food to the community, as, ever so subtly, Kurosawa suggests that for all their nobility even these samurai belong to an ethos of war and killing which ultimately does the society no good. Kurosawa has observed, in defence of the obvious disparity in terms of the author's sympathy between samurai and peasants, that throughout his large body of work he has demonstrated a sympathy for the oppressed, even for the kidnapper, Yamazai, in *High and Low*: 'it came naturally to me to be sympathetic toward an oppressed person', he said, indicating that this was why he chose Schubert's *Trout Quintet* as the musical motif assigned to this character.

Elsewhere in his writing Sato addresses *Seven Samurai*, but only to blame Kurosawa and the film itself with its presumptive approval of military power. *Seven Samurai*, Sato has written, in a polemical stretch, 'justified the Japanese rearmament; in 1954 the National Safety Force and Maritime Safety Board were reorganized into the Self-Defense Force (*Jietai*) in apparent violation of Article 9 of the 1947 constitution'. His view is no more outlandish, however, than an American of a similar bent. The guns of *Seven Samurai*, Frederick Kaplan writes in *Cinéaste* magazine, are symbols of Western imperialism. The mutual effort of peasants and samurai, Kaplan postulates, is an example of 'revolutionary solidarity'. In Kikuchiyo's planting of Heihachi's flag after his death, at that moment of stasis just before the bandits appear on the horizon, Kaplan discovers a 'tableau' which is 'reminiscent of socialist realism'. *Seven Samurai*, he concludes, is 'a reminder that the accomplishment of the samurai, men of action, and of the peasants, men of labor, will turn to dust unless the alliance between them progresses and develops'.

Yet the samurai are departing from the stage of history – by virtue of their being samurai there never was nor could ever be any such alliance. History and the structure of Japanese society made it unthinkable and the story Kurosawa tells in *Seven Samurai*, based as it is upon the historical detail that fallen samurai sometimes did work as watchmen or guards for peasants in exchange for meals, was an anomaly in Japanese history; it was a harbinger of the fall of the samurai rather than a promise that someday

Shino turns her shoulder away

peasants and samurai would make common political cause. Kaplan also contends that the ending of *Seven Samurai* is open: 'Whether Katsushiro remains with Shino in the village, whether the alliance between the peasants and the samurai continues, we do not know.' Here Kaplan need only have looked at the film; Shino, passing Katsushiro on her way to join the other farmers planting rice turns her shoulder away; he looks after her, but does not follow.

A much younger critic, Misuhiro Yoshimoto, has adopted Oshima's assessment of Kurosawa. Kurosawa's very enlistment of the *jidai-geki*, because it is a familiar Japanese genre, leads to his making his audience 'complicit' in 'the formation of Japan as a nation-state and even the home-grown imperialism of modern Japan', this notwithstanding Kurosawa's own anti-militarist political views.

In devaluing history, such critics simultaneously ignore irony. The greatness of *Seven Samurai* rests, in part, on its central ironic paradox. The unique selflessness, the goodness of the six samurai meets throughout the film the paradox that the entire class – the good along with the worst elements, represented by the forty bandits – is becoming obsolete. The transitory survival of three samurai is met by the pathos of historical defeat. The director's pain resides in a paradox: that the worthy must disappear along with the villainous.

Yoshimoto quotes a critic named Takeo Kuwabara who, like Sato and Tada, also insists that the real-life peasants of the fifteenth and sixteenth centuries were not as meek and fearful as Kurosawa depicts them. He also speculates, with Yoshimoto's approval, that 'in reality Kanbei [sic] would have become a lord of the village, and Katsushiro would have kept Shino as his mistress'. This view seems to me to be entirely contrary to Kurosawa's spirit, the humility with which he invests Kambei, the uprightness which Katsushiro has embraced as his samurai legacy. A general discomfort characterises writing about *Seven Samurai* in the decades since its release, both in Japan and abroad. Its cause may well be Kurosawa's innocent if no less profound acknowledgment of the influence of history in shaping consciousness, and the recalcitrance of class distinctions which inevitably separate individuals inexorably, regardless of good will.

Other recent critics, like Stephen Prince, in a book called *The Warrior's Camera: The Cinema of Akira Kurosawa*, insist that Kurosawa is suggesting that class distinctions are not so important after all. 'The warrior class had much more freedom at that time,' he writes ahistorically. 'A peasant could still become a warrior then.' Prince insists that Kurosawa is depicting 'the permeability of class lines', ignoring, entirely, the ending of the film, and the irony of Kikuchiyo's becoming the 'seventh' samurai. He adds to Kurosawa's perspective the myth that individual heroism is dependent upon an annihilation of the 'social construction of the self'.

Prince believes that Kambei's cutting his topknot and casting aside temporarily his sword in that early scene bespeak 'an apparent rejection of social codes'. Yet whatever the outward accoutrements, Kambei remains demonstrably and forever a samurai, the noble embodiment of those codes. He believes that Kambei's selfless act is 'far beyond the capability of the ordinary samurai', even as Kurosawa suggests that Kambei is being, precisely, a samurai in his discipline and his self-containment. Finally Prince thinks that Kurosawa sought to defeat history, as if such a thing were possible. This unreal aspiration was not Kurosawa's.

Prince also chastises Kurosawa for his influence on the Hollywood cinema, in particular, the Western. It is as if Kurosawa were responsible for the crass Western remakes of his films – *The Magnificent Seven* (1960) and *Fistful of Dollars* (1964) in particular. As Sato has rightly pointed out, any comparison between Kurosawa's *jidai-geki* and Hollywood Westerns is essentially meaningless: 'There is no distinction in the rank of characters who appear in westerns. The sheriff, outlaw, cowboy, farmer, etc. are more or less on an equal social footing.' Such films could be no more than parodies of Kurosawa's.

The differences between Kurosawa's *jidai-geki* in general, and *Seven Samurai* in particular, and the American Western film override any

The Magnificent Seven

surface similarities. The American Western – if ambiguously, as Sato has noted – looks forward to Western expansion and manifest destiny, a theme as apparent in *The Searchers* as in *McCabe and Mrs. Miller*. This theme is utterly absent in Japanese cinema. American Westerns also reveal an ambivalence towards technology; the railroad arrives in Shinbone simultaneously with the extinction of good men like Tom Doniphon in *The Man Who Shot Liberty Valance*.

Jidai-geki do not glorify the landscape. The theme of duty versus inclination, which pervades all of Japanese cinema, rarely surfaces in the American Western. If Shane departs, out of duty not to destroy an intact marriage, as well as to preserve his own freedom, there is no conflict about it. All the good people in *Red River* do what they must – it is both their inclination and their duty.

Nowhere are these differences more apparent than in John Sturges' remake of *Seven Samurai*, *The Magnificent Seven*. There are many scenes and dialogue which are virtual carbon copies of Kurosawa's original. The Kikuchiyo character played by Horst Buchholz in an important moment asks, 'who made us the way we are?' He answers his own question, 'men with guns', and concludes, 'so what do you expect us to be?' A scene in town chronicles the rounding up of gunfighters for the task. The alarm is sounded to bring the peasants out to greet the gunfighters. Scouts arrive and must be eliminated. An elder is given Kambei's closing lines, 'only the farmers have won', adding, tendentiously, 'they remain forever. They are like the land itself …'

Kurosawa's persistent visual use of the wind here is tamed into dialogue as the old man tells the survivors, 'you are like the wind, blowing over the land and passing on'. The Kambei character played by Yul Brynner adds, 'only the farmers won. We lost. We'll always lose.' It would appear as if this remake were faithful in both the letter and the spirit to Kurosawa's masterpiece.

Yet the confusion of equating samurai with American gunfighters, drifters of no particular function in the community, soon converts the film into an embarrassment. Sturges' gunfighters were a rabble, lower in both status and character than his sentimentalised Mexican campesinos. That being a samurai was a matter of birth, that you didn't choose to be a samurai, and that this station brought moral obligations of a higher order escapes him entirely.

Ironically, it is the bandit Calvera, played by Eli Wallach, who raises the issue of people who are 'not satisfied with their station in life', suggesting that class inequity contributes to the misery of the farmers.

This note is not sounded again in the film. The motivation of the evil has nothing to do with the structure of society, but with simple greed, whereas in Kurosawa the changes in the social order contribute in no small degree to *ronin* being driven to become outlaws.

Were these gunfighters to disappear, without Yul Brynner (with an atrocious accent that suggests nothing of the American West) and McQueen, the world would continue quite well. They have contributed little beyond the battle in the film; the significance of their acts nowhere extends outward to larger questions. If they have helped this village, it is but an aberration for them, and they are unlikely to do it again. Nor do they reveal qualities beyond gunfighting skill and a certain cleverness. As personalities none is remotely interesting; no one's character could fascinate anyone as Kambei's intrigues Gorobei. James Coburn, imitating Miyaguchi's performance as Kyuzo – laconic, lethal, swift, unsentimental – comes closest. There is even a virtually identical scene to *Seven Samurai* where he sits under a tree and examines a (cactus) flower as he waits for the three scouts.

Horst Buchholz, sporting a German accent, is ludicrous as Kikuchiyo: he lacks that character's daring, and the sense that he will have nothing to which to return when all this is over. Sturges collapses the apprentice Katsushiro and Kikuchiyo into one character – he has little interest in Kurosawa's master–teacher theme. Because the issue of class plays no role in this film, he allows *his* Katsushiro to remain in the village at the end. Indeed, why not, since the theme of the unique and impermeable samurai identity which cannot cross class lines is entirely missing. Mere sentiment and a romantic ending are substituted for complexity, irony and historical truth.

Some peasants refuse to fight, like Mosuke in his refusal to sacrifice his house for the good of the group. And even as Mosuke reversed his position, these peasants finally join the fray. Sturges does not bother, however, to articulate the theme of selflessness, so un-American and so alien to the theme of westward expansion. The gunfighter who joined because of the possibility of gold or silver mines is killed off early, but any discussion of the futility of living selfishly for material goals is absent.

Gone as well is the philosophic discussion of the relationship between the desires of the individual and the imperatives of the group. This entire conflict is vulgarised into a question of courage versus cowardice, the tired machismo of the American B-Western.

Near the close of the film, Sturges attempts to offer a justification for the life of the gunfighter, a version of its own transcendence. Steve

McQueen has enumerated the costs of this way of life: 'home none, wife none, kids none, prospects zero'. It seems a hard life to have chosen merely to call bartenders by their first name. Brynner replies: 'Places you're tied down to – none. People with a hold on you – none. Men you step aside for – none.'

Here the analogy between Kurosawa's *jidai-geki* and its pale American imitation completely breaks down. The samurai as *ronin*, like gunfighters, might be hired. But those conditions of life which Brynner finds desirable would be anathema to a samurai. A true samurai wanted nothing more than to be attached to a *daimyo* and a castle, to be 'tied down' in classic feudal organisation. That your lord had 'a hold on you' was both natural and good; that you 'stepped aside' for him was appropriate and natural, just as others stepped aside for you. 'Insults swallowed,' Vaughn adds, 'none.' This might well be true, but not the absence of 'enemies'. In fact, Vaughn did have enemies, those from whom he was fleeing. Samurai, however, saw their enemies, rival warlords and their samurai, as part of the inevitable and welcome landscape.

Brynner remains in the village when he might leave because 'we took a contract', and those unenforceable by law are precisely 'the kind we've got to keep'. The samurai fought out of the kindness and alliance with the land which justified, for Kurosawa, their entire birthright. The very mention of money and gratitude betray the spirit of *Seven Samurai*; the samurai code forbad the very touching of money as beneath a samurai's dignity.

At the heart of the impossibility of translating a *jidai-geki* to the American West is the theme of choice. The samurai even by law could not become farmers, or, as McQueen suggests, cattle ranchers. Katsushiro, young as he is, must play out the fate of his class. The entire pathos is lost if the gunfighters could have offered their superior strength to the community on a regular basis, if their overriding motivation was the common good: why didn't they then do just that?

One must also treat sceptically the view expressed by critic David Desser in *The Samurai Films of Akira Kurosawa* that Kurosawa has been 'influenced by Western, specifically American, popular formulas' in particular. The wide variety of films Kurosawa saw as he came of age alone belies this point. The list is catholic and broad. A partial catalogue, compiled by Kurosawa in his *Autobiography*, includes *The Cabinet Of Dr Caligari*; Fritz Lang's *Dr Mabuse*; most of Chaplin and Griffith; G.W. Pabst's *The Joyless Street*; Jean Renoir's *Nana*; Murnau's *Faust*; Lang's *Metropolis*; Eisenstein's *Potemkin*; Pudovkin's *Mother* and *Storm Over*

Asia; Carl Dreyer's *La Passion de Jeanne d'Arc*; Josef von Sternberg's *The Blue Angel*; Luis Buñuel's *Un Chien andalou*; and along with them some Japanese films like Daisuke Ito's *Chuji tabi nikki* and *Shinpan Ooka Seidan* and Minoru Murato's *Kaijin*. Included on the list Kurosawa specified in his *Autobiography* are also John Ford's *The Iron Horse* and *Three Bad Men*.

Questions of whether Kurosawa influenced Western films – or that they influenced him – are irrelevant to understanding him as a film-maker. No doubt there is some truth in both of these propositions, although neither leads to a stronger appreciation of his unique achievement. Kurosawa had remarked that it is 'because I am making films for today's young Japanese that I should find a Western-looking format the most practical'. From this, Desser concludes that Kurosawa's 'stated intention' was 'to make films in the Western style for Japanese audiences', which is a far cry from Kurosawa's hesitant 'Western-looking'. In fact, the cumulative episodic approach Kurosawa uses, the slowly gathering narrative style, is far more a Japanese than an Aristotelian or Western structure. Desser chooses *Throne of Blood* (1957) as Kurosawa's masterpiece because it takes 'man' out of a context, as if this were desirable.

In a vigorous effort to rescue *Seven Samurai* from the history which is its theme, Desser locates the episode of Kambei disguising himself as a priest in a Zen legend related by D.T. Suzuki. Ise no Kami had his head shaved, borrowed a robe and went to the rescue with lunch boxes, just as Kambei uses rice balls. That the episode is reflected in this story for Desser 'transform[s] *Seven Samurai* into the realm of legend'. In his effort to see the film as 'myth' rather than history, he concludes that the farmers were the winners because 'nature' triumphs at the end, as if the film were an agrarian fairy-tale. He decides that Kurosawa's intention was to convert history into myth. He quotes Roland Barthes's dubious assertion that 'myth has the task of giving an historical intention natural justification', precisely what Kurosawa avoids. It is one thing to reflect on the effect of history, another to applaud its inevitability. 'Myth is constituted by the loss of the historical quality of things,' he continues, something which never happens in *Seven Samurai*, down to the final shot. Even less appropriate to the perception of *Seven Samurai* is the final triumph of myth: 'Myth deprives the object of which it speaks of all History. In it, history evaporates.'

Desser reflects a bias which is not Kurosawa's own, that myth occupies a higher place in the intellectual pantheon than history. A 'mythicization of history' is what Kurosawa has achieved in *Seven Samurai*, he insists – one filled with 'iconic stereotypes'. One fact deters

Desser. He notices that while the sword is the icon of the *jidai-geki*, many – like Kurosawa's *Yojimbo*, *Sanjuro* and *Red Beard* – are set in the Tokugawa period, a time of peace. This irony, of course, is precisely the point. Desser is reduced to categorising *Seven Samurai* as a 'nostalgic samurai film', mistaking the edge and anger of its finish, as well as the cruelty in the visuals as the peasants ignore the samurai and the samurai await a bleak future. For good measure he throws into the pot the contention that 'the Samurai film can be seen as a Marxist formulation wherein the Proletariat are inevitably to triumph after a series of dialectical struggles against various ruling classes'.

One returns to Donald Richie's writing about Kurosawa. In his chapter on *Seven Samurai*, Richie focuses, modestly, on the 'magical images' of this film. He writes that Kurosawa 'has given us beauty in the midst of knowledge'. In his 1971 *Japanese Cinema*, he again calls *Seven Samurai* Kurosawa's 'best' film and 'one which, were it necessary to make the choice, I should call the finest Japanese film ever made'. Richie allows this judgment to stand in the 1982 revised edition of *The Japanese Film: Art and Industry*, which he wrote with Joseph L. Anderson in 1959: *Seven Samurai* is 'among the best films ever made not only in Japan but anywhere in the world'.

The three surviving samurai after the battle, in the heavy rain

The Epic Moment: Kurosawa's Controversial Ending

The ending of *Seven Samurai* actually begins in the penultimate sequence, creating a metaphoric match-on-action. From a high angle, the three surviving samurai are left in the heavy rain. Kambei and his sidekick, Shichiroji, stand, exhausted; Katsushiro is on his knees in the water, weeping.

'Again we've survived,' Kambei says. There is a cut to the flag Heihachi sewed, still blowing. A horse neighs, in reprise. The wind blows dust and earth into the air, like smoke, lifting the film out of the moment in the sixteenth century in which it is set, into all of history. There is a deep fade. The rest of the conversation will occur in the coming scene.

The sounds of the farmers singing begin beneath the fade, the sound of their triumph bleeding through. The fade-in to the final scene is in bright sunlight. The farmers sing as they plant. Rikichi beats a drum and prances in contentment, as if his bitterness at the loss of his wife has been washed away at last. Manzo plays a bamboo flute, having reconciled himself to the transgression of his daughter. All is now right in the world of these characters.

There is, at first, no sign of the samurai, which is fitting. Then they appear, standing on a bridge, just as Kikuchiyo died on a bridge. The camera is quickly raised to a higher angle so that it looks down on Rikichi, as if, despite his joy, he is, finally, a lesser character on the historical stage. His selfishness, after all, a wilful, if understandable, emotion, cost Heihachi his life. The moral power of the film shifts to the samurai for the last time. As soon as he cuts to Katsushiro, Kurosawa alters perspective to

Rikichi beats a drum and prances in contentment

a low angle looking upward, an angle of respect for the youngest of the samurai, now, as Kambei called him, 'a full-fledged man'.

Kambei turns and walks away from the spectacle of singing, planting farmers. Shichiroji and Katsushiro follow. Without a word of dialogue Kurosawa conveys that there is no longer a place for them here in this village where their friends have lost their lives. Instead, they stand before the graves, which represent both their future and the destiny of their entire class. The graves presage, as well, the loss of all the values for which they stand.

The entire scene renounces realism, and demonstrates yet again that this action film transcends the stylistic category into which critics have placed it. Rather, the final scene is a reminder that *Seven Samurai* is deeply stylised, a ballet addressing the meaning of the history hitherto portrayed.

Shino passes carrying her plants, on her way to join the others. Katsushiro steps forward. His eyes meet hers. But she does not stop, and if he follows, it is only for a few steps. She joins the line of women planting, while Katsushiro remains on the bridge to his doomed future, although he is very young, having only just become that 'full-fledged man', as Kambei had joked. They say nothing to each other. Her singing is very loud, as if to drown out forever whatever she might have felt. Even as the samurai class is fading, it is, finally, inconceivable that Katsushiro should ally himself with a farmer's daughter.

There are still no words uttered as Shichiroji turns to Kambei. The chief steps forward, his arms folded across his chest. 'Again we're defeated,' he says. 'Huh?' Shichiroji utters in a sound of protest. Haven't they just killed every bandit; hasn't the village been returned to order?

Shino sings as if to drown out forever what she might have felt

The samurai on the bridge, looking towards the planting farmers

Kambei speaks to Schichiroji: 'Again we're defeated'

With the death of the samurai, an entire world has been extinguished

'The winners are those farmers. Not us,' Kambei says. He turns to face the graves, in the most dramatic tableau of the film, one standing for Kurosawa's own mourning of the demise of the samurai class. As the three men look upward, the camera lifts to reframe the shot, so that all that is left are the four graves above, and the scattered peasant graves below.

Over the last shot, devoid of human habitation, the wind blows hard under the samurai musical motif. It grows even louder, heralding both the beauty of these men and their demise. The music crescendos in defiance of the inevitable. Into each of the four samurai graves have been placed, as tradition so demanded, both the long sword and the short, symbols of samurai pride and identity.

The villains have been defeated and yet this is a deeply sad ending, for the samurai have won the battle, but lost the war. These good and noble men have outlived their time, an inordinate loss for Japan. The farmers survive, but their legacy is one of self-interest. Despite the sacrifice these samurai have made for them, just as the samurai were not welcomed when they arrived, so, despite the courageous war they waged, no one has uttered a word of gratitude or even shows any awareness of their presence. They are as 'selfish' as Kikuchiyo said they were. They are as 'stupid' too, a theme which began when during the threshing it seemed as if the bandits were not to return and then some of the farmers began to complain about 'greedy' samurai. Nor have the samurai expected gratitude. They have turned their backs on the villagers to face the graves of their four fallen comrades.

The final fade bespeaks austerity, a dirge for the spirit of Japan which will never again be so strong, so purposeful, so full of dignity and grace. With the death of the samurai, an entire world has been extinguished. It is to the samurai class, epitomised by these men – those surviving, a very temporary condition, and those dead – that Kurosawa pays his final homage.

Seven Samurai at the last becomes an elegy, a window into Akira Kurosawa's heart. From the vantage of the post-war moment, he mourns how and when Japan lost its best self. The history which followed would for him move in an ever downward moral direction.

CREDITS
. . . .
Shichinin No Samurai/Seven Samurai

Japan
1954

Production Company
Toho Co. Ltd
Producer
Shojiro Motoki
Director
Akira Kurosawa
Assistant Director
Hiromichi Horikawa
Screenplay
Akira Kurosawa, Shinobu
Hashimoto, Hideo Oguni
Director of Photography
Asaichi Nakai
Lighting
Shigeru Mori
Art Director
So Matsuyama
Art Consultants
Seiton Maeda, Kohei Ezaki
Music
Fumio Hayasaka
Archery Directors
Ienori Kaneko,
Shigeru Endo
Sound Recordist
Fumio Yanoguchi

Cast
Takashi Shimura
Kambei, leader of samurai
Toshiro Mifune
Kikuchiyo,
would-be samurai
Seiji Miyaguchi
Kyuzo, swordsman
Ko Kimura
Katsushiro, young samurai
Daisuke Kato
Shichiroji, Kambei's friend
Minoru Chiaki
Heihachi, good-natured
samurai
Yoshio Inaba
Gorobei, wise warrior
Yoshio Tsuchiya
Rikichi, militant villager
Keiko Tsushima
Shino, village girl
Kamatari Fujiwara
Manzo, Shino's father
Bokuzen Hidari
Yohei, frightened villager
Kuninori Kodo
Gisaku, village elder
Yoshio Kosugi
Mosuke
Keiji Sakakida
Gosaku
Fumiko Homma
peasant woman
Sojin Kamiyama
minstrel priest
Toranosuke Ogawa
grandfather
Yu Akitsu
husband
Noriko Sengoku
wife
Ichiro Chiba
priest
Gen Shimizu
masterless samurai
Jun Tatari
coolie

Atsushi Watanabe
vendor
Yukiko Shimazaki
Rikichi's wife
Shimpei Takagi
bandit chief
Jiro Kumagai
Haruko Toyama
Tsuneo Katagiri
Yasuhisa Tsutsumi
peasants
Kichijiro Ueda
Akira Tani
Haruo Nakajima
Takashi Narita
Senkichi Omura
Shuno Takahara
Masanobu Okubo
bandits
Tatsuya Nakadai

Black and White
14,000 feet
200 minutes

Japanese premiere
26 April 1954

Credits compiled
by Markku Salmi,
BFI Filmographic Unit.

Seven Samurai is available
in the UK from BFI Video:
DVD cat. no. BFID 501,
VHS cat. no. CR 220.

BIBLIOGRAPHY

. . . .

Akira Kurosawa, ed. Michael Esteve, *Etudes Cinématographiques* nos. 30–31, Spring 1964.

Anderson, Joseph L., and Donald Richie, *The Japanese Film: Art and Industry* (New York: Grove Press, 1960; expanded edition, Princeton, NJ: Princeton University Press, 1982).

Bock, Audie, *Japanese Film Directors* (Tokyo and New York: Kodansha International, 1978).

Burch, Noël, *To the Distant Observer: Form and Meaning in the Japanese Cinema* (Berkeley: University of California Press, 1979).

Desser, David, *The Samurai Films of Akira Kurosawa* (Ann Arbor, MI: UMI Research Press, 1983).

Eisenstein, S.M., *Film Form: Essays in Film Theory*, trans. by Jay Leyda (New York: Meridian, 1958).

Goodwin, James, *Akira Kurosawa and Intertextual Cinema* (Baltimore, MD: Johns Hopkins University Press, 1994).

Hall, John Whitney, *Japan: From Prehistory to Modern Times* (New York: Delta, 1970).

Hane, Mikiso, *Japan: A Historical Survey* (New York: Charles Scribner's Sons, 1972).

Kaplan, Frederick, 'A Second Look: Akira Kurosawa's *Seven Samurai*', *Cinéaste*, vol. 10 no. 68, Winter 1979/80, pp. 42–43, 47.

Kracauer, Siegfried, *Theory of Film: The Redemption of Physical Reality* (New York: Oxford University Press, 1960).

Kurosawa, Akira, *Something Like an Autobiography* (New York: Alfred A. Knopf, 1982).

Mellen, Joan, 'The Epic Cinema of Kurosawa', *Take One* vol. 3 no. 4, 1972, pp. 16–19.

———, *Voices from the Japanese Cinema* (New York: Liveright, 1975).

———, *The Waves at Genji's Door: Japan Through Its Cinema* (New York: Pantheon, 1976).

Oshima, Nagisa, *Cinema, Censorship and the State: The Writings of Nagisa Oshima* (Cambridge, MA: MIT Press, 1992).

Prince, Stephen, *The Warrior's Cinema: The Cinema of Akira Kurosawa* (Princeton, NJ: Princeton University Press, 1991).

Richie, Donald, *The Films of Akira Kurosawa* (Berkeley: University of California Press, 1965; 2nd edition, with supplementary material by Joan Mellen, 1984).

———, *Japanese Cinema: Film Style and National Character* (New York: Anchor, 1971).

———, *Ozu* (Berkeley: University of California Press, 1974).

Sansom, George, *A History of Japan, 1334–1615* (Stanford, CA: Stanford University Press, 1961).

Sato, Tadao, *Currents in Japanese Cinema* (Tokyo and New York: Kodansha International, 1982).

The Seven Samurai: Modern Film Scripts (New York: Simon and Schuster, 1970).

Tucker, Richard N., *Japan: Film Image* (London: Studio Vista, 1973).

Yoshimoto, Mitsuhiro, *Kurosawa: Film Studies and Japanese Cinema* (Durham, NC: Duke University Press, 2000).

ALSO PUBLISHED

An Actor's Revenge
Ian Breakwell

L'Âge d'or
Paul Hammond

L'Année dernière à Marienbad
Jean-Louis Leutrat

Annie Hall
Peter Cowie

L'Atalante
Marina Warner

L'avventura
Geoffrey Nowell-Smith

Belle de Jour
Michael Wood

The Big Heat
Colin McArthur

The Big Sleep
David Thomson

The Birds
Camille Paglia

Blackmail
Tom Ryall

Bonnie and Clyde
Lester D. Friedman

Boudu Saved from Drowning
Richard Boston

Bride of Frankenstein
Alberto Manguel

Brief Encounter
Richard Dyer

Das Cabinet des Dr. Caligari
David Robinson

Cat People
Kim Newman

Chinatown
Michael Eaton

Citizen Kane
Laura Mulvey

Double Indemnity
Richard Schickel

Les Enfants du paradis
Jill Forbes

42nd Street
J. Hoberman

"Fires Were Started –"
Brian Winston

The Ghost and Mrs Muir
Frieda Grafe

Greed
Jonathan Rosenbaum

Gun Crazy
Jim Kitses

High Noon
Phillip Drummond

In a Lonely Place
Dana Polan

It's a Gift
Simon Louvish

The Life and Death of Colonel Blimp
A. L. Kennedy

Lolita
Richard Corliss

M
Anton Kaes

The Magnificent Ambersons
V. F. Perkins

A Matter of Life and Death
Ian Christie

Meet Me in St. Louis
Gerald Kaufman

Metropolis
Thomas Elsaesser

Napoléon
Nelly Kaplan

The Night of the Hunter
Simon Callow

La Nuit américaine
Roger Crittenden

Odd Man Out
Dai Vaughan

Olympia
Taylor Downing

Palm Beach Story
John Pym

Pépé le Moko
Ginette Vincendeau

Performance
Colin MacCabe

Queen Christina
Marcia Landy & Amy Villarejo

Red River
Suzanne Liandrat-Guigues

Rocco and his Brothers
Sam Rohdie

Rome Open City
David Forgacs

Sanshô Dayû
Dudley Andrew & Carole Cavanaugh

The Searchers
Edward Buscombe

The Seventh Seal
Melvyn Bragg

Shadows
Ray Carney

Shane
Edward Countryman & Evonne von Heussen-Countryman

Singin' in the Rain
Peter Wollen

Stagecoach
Edward Buscombe

Sunrise – A Song of Two Humans
Lucy Fischer

Taxi Driver
Amy Taubin

Things to Come
Christopher Frayling

Went the Day Well?
Penelope Houston

Wild Strawberries
Philip & Kersti French

The Wizard of Oz
Salman Rushdie

If you would like further information about future BFI Film Classics or about other books on film, media and popular culture from BFI Publishing, please write to:

BFI Film Classics
BFI Publishing
21 Stephen Street
London W1P 2LN

BFI Film Classics '...could scarcely be improved upon ... informative, intelligent, jargon-free companions.'
The Observer

Each book in the BFI Publishing Film Classics series honours a great film from the history of world cinema. With new titles published each year, the series is rapidly building into a collection representing some of the best writing on film. If you would like to receive further information about future Film Classics or about other books on film, media and popular culture from BFI Publishing, please fill in your name and address and return this card to the BFI.* (No stamp required if posted in the UK, Channel Islands, or Isle of Man.)

NAME _____

ADDRESS _____

_____

_____

POSTCODE _____

WHICH *BFI FILM CLASSIC* DID YOU BUY? _____

_____

* In North America, please return your card to: Indiana University Press, Attn: LPB, 601 N. Morton Street, Bloomington, IN 47401-3797

21

BFI Publishing
21 Stephen Street
FREEPOST 7
LONDON
W1E 4AN